# PROPHETS IN THE QUR'AN

## Volume Two

## The Later Prophets

Iftekhar Bano Hussain

Ta-Ha Publishers Ltd

Reprint 1998

Published by
**Ta-Ha Publishers Ltd.**
1, Wynne Road
London SW9 OBB
website:http://www.taha.co.uk/
email: sales@taha.co.uk



Edited and Typeset by Ahmad Thomson

British Library Cataloguing in Publication Data

Hussain, Iftekhar Bano
Prophets in the Qur'an - Volume Two: The Later Prophets
1. Islam.
I. Title

**ISBN 1 897940 29 7**

Printed and Bound in Great Britain by:
De-Luxe Printers,
London NW10 7NR.
website: http://www.de-luxe.com

بسم الله الرحمن الرحيم

IN THE NAME OF ALLAH
THE MERCIFUL THE COMPASSIONATE

# DEDICATION

This book is dedicated to whoever
recites and studies the Qur'an,
and to those from among the People of the Book
who have had the good fortune to recognise the Prophet
Muhammad, may Allah bless him and grant him peace,
and to embrace Islam.

شجرة نسب الأنبياء عليهم السلام
رسول الله
Muhammad
صلى الله عليه وسلم
فاطمة
رقية
عبد الله
زينب
أم كلثوم
'Ali
'Umar
Uthm an
Abu Bakr
عبد الله
عبد المطلب
هاشم
عبد مناف
قصي
كلاب
مرة
كعب
لؤي
غالب
فهر
مالك
نضر
كنانة
خزيمة
مدركة
الياس
مضر
نزار
معد
عدنان
Yusuf
Ya'qub
Musa
Harun
Shu'aib
Lut
Isma'il
Ishaq
Ibrahim
هاران
Dhu'l Kifl
'Isa ibn Maryam
Ayyub
Nuh
Idris
شيث
Salih
Hud
Ilyas
Yahya
Zakariyya
Da'ud
Sulayman
Alyassa'
هابيل
قابيل
Adam
أبو البشر
منها خلقناكم وفيها نعيدكم ومنها نخرجكم تارة أخرى
المدينة المنورة
يا أيها الناس اتقوا ربكم الذي خلقكم من نفس واحدة وخلق منها زوجها وبث منهما رجالا كثيرا ونساء واتقوا الله الذي تساءلون به والأرحام إن الله كان عليكم رقيبا

# CONTENTS

# About the Author

Iftekhar Bano Hussain was born in Nagpur, India. During her schooling she attended both a Muslim Middle School and a Christian High School, and as a result her comparative studies of the Qur'an and the Bible, which have continued throughout her life, commenced at an early age. Having been granted a Masters Degree from Nagpur University in 1950, she migrated with her husband to Karachi, Pakistan. After being granted a B.Ed. Degree from Karachi University in 1952, Mrs. Hussain was awarded a scholarship for postgraduate studies in education and teacher training in London, England, where both she and her husband, a qualified engineer, spent five years, before returning to Pakistan.

As well as devoting her care and time primarily to her growing family but also to her career, Mrs Hussain became interested in palmistry and studied it extensively. When, however, she went with her two sons on 'Umra to Makka in 1971, followed by a visit to Madina, she lost all interest in palmistry, and intensified her study of the Qur'an instead. Since then, Mrs Hussain has subsequently visited the Haramayn on seven further occasions.

On one of those occasions, in Dhu'l-Hijjah 1397/1977, Mrs Hussain had the good fortune to climb the Jebel an-Nur up to the cave of Hira, where the Prophet Muhammad, may Allah bless him and grant him peace, first received revelation of the Qur'an from the angel Jibril, peace be on him. The cave is small, barely large enough to accommodate one person, and near the mouth of the cave there is a flat space which is just large enough for one person to do the prayer – which Mrs Hussain clearly remembers doing, with the Ka'ba in sight, far down in the valley of Makka below.

Mrs Hussain has written several books in both Urdu and English, including books for children and some poetry. As well as her books on *Prophets in the Qur'an*, her revised edition of *Astonishing Truths of the Holy Qur'an* and her *History of Islam*, again both in Urdu and in English, are currently being prepared for publication.

# FOREWORD

This book, *Prophets in the Qur'an – Volume Two,* is the sequel to *Prophets in the Qur'an – Volume One.* Whereas *Volume One* considers all the major Prophets mentioned in the Qur'an from the first Prophet to appear on earth, *sayyedina* Adam up to and including *sayyedina* Shu'aib, *Volume Two* considers all the major Prophets mentioned in the Qur'an from *sayyedina* Musa up to and including *sayyedina* 'Isa, the last Prophet to appear on earth before the coming of the Last Prophet, *sayyedina* Muhammad, may the blessings and peace of Allah be on him and on all the Prophets – and on all the sincere followers of all the Prophets.

Everything that was stated in the Foreword to *Volume One* applies equally to *Volume Two* and need not be repeated again in the pages which follow.

The significance of the Prophets whose lives are considered in *Volume Two,* is that probably more than half the world's population claims to be following one or another of them – the Jews claim to be following *sayyedina* Musa, peace be on him; the Christians claim to be following *sayyedina* 'Isa, peace be on him; and the Muslims claim to be following *sayyedina* Muhammad, may Allah bless him and grant him peace.

In spite of the fact that these three great Prophets were sent by the same and only God, with basically the same message – and in spite of the fact that they each told their followers about each other during their own lifetimes – anyone who came to this world from another world today might easily come to the conclusion that the three major religions of Judaism, Christianity and Islam are three very different religions which, in spite of any similarities they might share, are nevertheless three mutually exclusive religions. Alternatively, our visitor from another world might conclude – since the followers of each of these religions account for the differences between them by stating that the other two have to some extent got it wrong and that only they have the whole truth – that at least one of them, or else none of them, must be right!

This book sets out to summarise what the Qur'an has to say about this matter, and accordingly there is very little speculation or conjecture or personal opinion in the pages which follow. The author has simply tried to gather together all the relevant *ayat* concerning each of the Prophets in turn. Since there are so many *ayat* either describing or addressed directly to those who claim still to be following either *sayyedina* Musa or *sayyedina* 'Isa, peace be on them, there is also a separate chapter entitled *The People of the Book* which includes many but not all of these *ayat*.

One of the great achievements of the early Muslim scholars was the gathering together of the great collections of *hadith*, the eyewitness reports of what the Prophet Muhammad and his companions did and said, may the blessings and peace of Allah be on him and on his family and on his companions. These reports were often initially transmitted by word of mouth from one person to another, although there are instances of reports being written down at the time that the events or words which a *hadith* records either occurred or were spoken. Eventually all the *hadith* came to be written down.

At the same time that this was taking place, the science of assessing the accuracy and reliability of any particular *hadith* was also developed by the Muslim scholars, and this science was based principally on assessing the reliability of the person or persons transmitting the *hadith* – the chain of transmission, or *isnad* as it is called in Arabic – as well as on whether or not the same *hadith* may have been transmitted by more than one chain of transmission.

There was also a different kind of transmission, which was that of behavioural transmission. To take one obvious example, the companions of the Prophet Muhammad, may Allah bless him and grant him peace, learned how to do the prayer by watching and imitating him as well as by listening to his verbal instructions. After his death, the people who became the companions of the people who had been his companions learned how to do the prayer from them by means of exactly the same process – and so on up to the present day. This kind of transmission is known as the transmission of *amal* – of action – and applies to all behaviour.

As with the written word, so with the transmission of human behaviour, some chains of transmission were more accurate and more reliable than others – for there is always the possibility that someone will change or invent or standardise what is being passed on, thereby altering the original form in some way. Thus whoever has been given the permission by his or her teacher to teach others has always been considered more reliable by people who possess discernment, especially if the teachers in question ultimately trace back to the Prophet Muhammed, may Allah bless him and grant him peace, and especially if all these teachers were noted for their fear and love of Allah and His Messenger and for the extent and depth of their knowledge of the Qur'an and the *deen* of Islam and life itself.

It is significant, when we consider the teachings of *sayyedina* Musa and *sayyedina* 'Isa, that these two kinds of transmission – whether of the written word or of action – have not survived the passage of time into the present age, even as regards the actual revelations which each of these two Prophets were given.

As was pointed out in the *Foreword* to *Volume One*, the Muslims confirm and respect the truth and accuracy of the earlier revelations which preceded the Qur'an, while recognising that today's Bible does not contain the original revelations of Musa, Da'ud and 'Isa, peace be on them, but rather versions of them that have been written and rewritten many times over by humans – along with numerous additions, subtractions and a lterations – and often hundreds of years after the original revelations were revealed.

Thus the Old Testament is comprised mainly of historical accounts by more than one author of what is said to have happened to the followers of Musa *after* his death, while the New Testament is comprised mainly of unauthenticated accounts of the life of 'Isa by people who never even met him. Although there are certainly elements of truth to be found in the Bible, the Old Testament does not contain the original Taurah which was revealed to the Prophet Musa, in the original pure Hebrew. The New Testament does not contain the original Ingil which was revealed to the Prophet 'Isa, in the original pure Aramaic.

Today only the Qur'an which was revealed to the Prophet Muhammad, may the blessings and peace of Allah be on all three of them, remains exactly as it was first revealed, in the language in which it was revealed, pure Arabic.

When it comes to the transmission of what *sayyedina* Musa and *sayyedina* 'Isa said and did while they were alive, then the record is even more blurred. Indeed it is at times so blurred that some Jews and Christians are unaware even of the need to distinguish between the Books which were revealed to *sayyedina* Musa and *sayyedina* 'Isa on one hand, and the recorded words and actions of the Prophets they claim to be following on the other.

The Muslims, on the other hand, have always been very careful to maintain the clear distinction that exists between what the Qur'an says on one hand, and what other people say they heard or saw the Prophet Muhammad say or do, on the other. Indeed while the Qur'an was being revealed, the Prophet Muhammad actually appointed some scribes to record it – and nothing but it – in writing.

It is because the *hadith* have been so scrupulously authenticated and assessed, and because they so often provide a reliable and illuminating contemporary record of what the Prophet Muhammad and his companions said and did, may the blessings and peace of Allah be on him and them, that whereas relatively few *hadith* are quoted in *Volume One*, far more *hadith* are quoted in *Volume Two* – although when compared to the total number of *hadith* that have actually been recorded, the number of *hadith* which are quoted in the pages which follow is very small indeed. Wherever possible only the most reliable of *hadith*, about which there can be no doubt whatsoever, have been quoted. In so doing, I have frequently made use of the renowned work of *Ash-Shifa'* of *Qadi* 'Iyad, whose extensive knowledge of both the Qur'an and the *hadith* literature was matched only by his scrupulous attention to detail and his insistence on relying only on fully authenticated *hadith*. As he himself says, in his extraordinary work, 'We have confined ourselves to those which are sound and well-known.'

I would also like to take this opportunity to acknowledge my gratitude to Hajj Abdal-Haqq and 'A'isha Abdarrahman Bewley whose translation of *Qadi* 'Iyad's work into English has made it accessible to all those whose knowledge of Arabic is limited. It is from this translation, published by Madinah Press, that the quotes from *Ash-Shifa'* which appear in this book are taken.

As well as utilising the sources to which reference has already been made in the Foreword to *Volume One*, constant use was also made during the writing of *Volume Two* to the *tafsirs* of Ibn Kathir, Yusuf Ali and Sayyid Abul A'la Mawdudi.

I have also included, within the context of the chapters which appear in *Volume Two*, an extremely brief historical account of how the groups who today are known as 'the Jews' and 'the Christians' first formed and came to be identified as such, and of how the religions of Judaism and Christianity came to be developed – given that the original followers of *sayyedina* Musa and *sayyedina* 'Isa were 'Muslims', that is, men and women who submitted their will to the Creator of the heavens and the earth – and that the original *deen* of both *sayyedina* Musa and *sayyedina* 'Isa, peace be on them, was not other than the *deen* of Islam, that is, the Prophetic way of life which is based on submitting to and worshipping the Source of all existence, Allah – Who said to all of His Messengers, may the blessings and peace of Allah be on all of them:

> **O Messengers, eat what is good and do good – surely I am aware of what you do – and surely this community of yours is one community, and I am your Lord, so have *taqwa* of Me. (23.51-52).**

And Who said to *sayyedina* Muhammad, may Allah bless him and grant him peace:

> **He has commanded you to follow the same *deen* that He decreed for Nuh, and which We have revealed to you (O Muhammad), and which We decreed for Ibrahim, and for Musa, and for 'Isa, saying, 'Establish the *deen* and do not become divided in it.'**

> **What you are calling the idol worshippers to follow is dreadful for them, but Allah chooses whomever He wishes for Himself, and He guides whoever turns to Him to Himself.**
>
> **And they did not become divided until after knowledge had come to them, out of rivalry amongst themselves, and if it had not been for a decree for an appointed term which had already come from your Lord, judgement concerning them would certainly have been passed – and surely those who have inherited the Book after them are hopelessly in doubt about it.**
>
> **So call them to that (*deen*) and go straight, as you have been commanded – and do not follow their desires, but say: 'I believe in whatever Book Allah has revealed, and I have been commanded to be just with you; Allah is our Lord and your Lord; we have our actions and you have your actions – so let there not be any argument between us and you; Allah will gather us together – and to Him is the journeying.' (42.13-15).**

It is important to understand the way in which the religions of Judaism and Christianity developed not simply because it is very interesting, but also especially because the Prophet Muhammad, may Allah bless him and grant him peace, warned that some of the Muslims would make the same mistakes as their predecessors – meaning the Jews and the Christians – bit by bit and step by step so that even if they were to crawl down a lizard's hole, these Muslims would follow them. (Al-Bukhari and Muslim).

It has been transmitted by 'Auf ibn Malik that the Prophet, may Allah bless him and grant him peace, said, 'The Jews split into seventy-one sects: one will enter Paradise and seventy will enter Hell. The Christians split into seventy-two sects: seventy-one will enter Hell and one will enter Paradise. By Him in Whose hand is my soul, my *Ummah* will split into seventy-three sects: one will enter Paradise and seventy-two will enter Hell.' Someone asked, 'O Messenger of Allah, who will they be?' He replied, 'The main body of the Muslims.' (Abu Da'ud).

In a similar *hadith* which has been recorded by At-Tirmidhi, when the Prophet was asked who would be the group of Muslims who were destined for the Garden, he replied, 'Those who base themselves on what I and my Companions are doing today.'

Accordingly it is not only necessary for Muslims to know how the Prophet Muhammad and his community lived – and to base their ownlives as closely as possible on that pattern – may the blessings and peace of Allah be on him, and on his family and his companions, and on all those who follow him and them with sincerity in what they are able until the Last day – but also it is extremely helpful for Muslims to understand what has been done to the original teachings of *sayyedina* Musa and *sayyedina* 'Isa, peace be on them, if they themselves are to avoid making the same mistakes and repeating the same patterns of action which have been made and followed by the Jews and the Christians.

The lesson to be learnt from the past is clear: in order to follow in the dust of the footsteps of *sayyedina* Muhammad, may Allah bless him and grant him peace, a believer cannot afford to worship the *shari'a* instead of Allah – which is what the Jews have tended to do; nor can a believer afford to worship the Messenger instead of the One Who sent him – which is what the Christians have tended to do; a believer can only afford to worship Allah by following the example of the Last Messenger, Muhammad, may Allah bless him and grant him peace:

> **O you who believe, believe in Allah, and in His Messenger, and in the Book which He has revealed to His Messenger, and in the Book which He revealed in the past – and as for whoever disbelieves in Allah, and in His angels, and in His Books, and in His Messengers, and in the Last Day, then he has indeed wandered far astray. (4.136).**

And:

> **Surely those who disbelieve in Allah and His Messengers, or who seek to make distinctions between Allah and His Messengers, and who say, 'We believe in some of them, but**

> **we do not believe in others, and so we seek to choose a course that lies between them,' these ones are in truth really disbelievers – and for the disbelievers We have prepared a humiliating punishment – but as for those who believe in Allah and His Messengers, and who do not make any distinction between any of them, He will certainly give these ones their reward – and Allah has always been Forgiving, Compassionate.** (4.150-152).

And:

> **Surely those who oppose Allah and His Messenger will certainly be humiliated. Allah has decreed: 'I will certainly be victorious – I and My Messengers – surely Allah is Powerful, Mighty.**
>
> **You will not find people who believe in Allah and the Last Day loving those who oppose Allah and His Messenger – even if they are their own fathers, or their sons, or their brothers, or their kindred.**
>
> **As for these, He has decreed that *iman* will be in their hearts, and He has strengthened them with a Spirit from Him, and He will bring them into Gardens underneath which rivers flow, in which they will dwell for ever.**
>
> **Allah is pleased with them and they are pleased with Him – it is these who are the party of Allah – and is it not the party of Allah who are the successful ones?** (58.20-22).

Whoever obeys Allah by following His Messenger will find his or her heart filled with peace and wisdom, whatever the difficulties and trials that may come on life's journey, and part of that wisdom will inevitably be an understanding of and a love not only for *sayyedina* Muhammad but for *all* of the Prophets, from Adam to Muhammad, may the blessings and peace of Allah be on all of them, for in whatever has come down to us about them, whether it be in the Qur'an or in the sayings of the Prophet Muhammad, there is a lesson to be learned and applied:

> **There is certainly a lesson in their history for people of understanding. It (the Qur'an) is not a story that has been made up, but a confirmation of what you already have, and an explanation of everything, and a guidance and a mercy for people who believe. (12.111).**

And whoever disobeys Allah by not following His Messenger will find his or her heart filled with turmoil and ignorance, and part of that ignorance will inevitably be a profound lack of understanding about the meaning and purpose of life, so that whatever life he or she leads will not ultimately be of any use:

> **Say: 'Shall we tell you who will be the greatest losers in what they do? – Those whose efforts in the life of this world go off course while they think that what they are doing is good.' These are the ones who disbelieve in the signs of their Lord and in the meeting with Him – and so their actions are of no use, and We will not give them any weight on the Day of Standing. That is their reward – Hell – because they disbelieved and treated Our signs and Our Messengers with scorn. As for those who believe and do good, surely the welcome of the Gardens of Paradise will be theirs, in which they will dwell for ever, never wishing to leave them.**
>
> **Say: 'Even if the sea became ink for the words of my Lord, then certainly the sea would run dry before the words of my Lord were exhausted,' – and even if We provided the same again to help!**
>
> **Say: 'I am only a human like you – it has been revealed to me that surely your God is One God, so let whoever looks forward to the meeting with his Lord do good deeds – and let him not associate any partner with Him in the worship of his Lord.' (18.103-110).**

And as Allah says:

> **I did not create the *jinn* and mankind except to worship Me.** (51.56).

It has been transmitted by 'Abdullah ibn 'Umar, may Allah be pleased with him, that the Prophet Muhammad, may Allah bless him and grant him peace, said, 'Convey my teachings to others, even if it is only a sentence, and you may relate *hadith* from the Tribe of Israel – for it is not wrong to do so – but whoever intentionally tells a lie and attributes it to me will certainly take his place in the Fire.' (Al-Bukhari).

# CHAPTER ONE

## THE PROPHET MUSA
### peace be on him

*Sayyedina* Musa was descended from one of the twelve sons of *sayyedina* Ya'qub – who was also known as Israel – whose descendants became known as the twelve tribes of the Tribe of Israel. *Sayyedina* Musa – whose father was called 'Imran – was descended from Levi, one of the eleven brothers of *sayyedina* Yusuf. Thus *sayyedina* Musa was born after the brothers of *sayyedina* Yusuf and their father *sayyedina* Ya'qub had settled in Egypt.

Indeed, by the time that *sayyedina* Musa came to be born, in about the 13th century BC, the Tribe of Israel had become a slave class in Egypt which was ruled by Firaoun – the Pharaoh – and his magicians. Like many of the great so-called civilisations before them, the society of Egypt at this time was very cultured and very ignorant. It was characterised by the use of magic – an art in which Firaoun's magicians were highly skilled.

The society of ancient Egypt at this time was formed in the same manner as the pyramids which its rulers made its people build using the Tribe of Israel as slave labour: At the top of the pyramid ruled Firaoun and his magicians; beneath them were carefully structured classes of people, whose degree of influence diminished the lower down they were in the invisible form of the pyramid; and at the bottom of society were the underclass – the slaves – whose cheap labour sustained the needs of everyone above them.

Like many of the great so-called civilisations before them, the majority of the people in Egypt at this time were idol worshippers – they worshipped whatever they perceived to be the source of power, not realising that Allah *is* the Source of all power.

Many people in this society, including Firaoun himself, believed that it was Firaoun who was all powerful, that it was he who was god, as these *ayat* from Surat an-Nazi'at indicate:

> **Has the story of Musa come to you? – How his Lord called to him in the sacred valley of Tuwa (saying), 'Go to Firaoun – surely he has exceeded the limits – and say, "Are you ready to purify yourself? Then I will guide you to your Lord, so that you fear Him."'**
>
> **So he (Musa) showed him (Firaoun) the great sign – but he denied and disobeyed and then hastily turned away and gathered (the people) together and made a proclamation – and he said, 'I am your lord the most high.'**
>
> **So Allah punished him, as an example in the next life and this life – surely in that there is indeed a lesson for whoever fears (his Lord). (79.15-26).**

It was into this society that *sayyedina* Musa, and his brother *sayyedina* Harun, peace be on them – who are known by the Jews and the Christians as the Prophet Moses and his brother Aaron – were born. The Qur'an makes it absolutely clear that both *sayyedina* Musa and *sayyedina* Harun were Prophets:

> **And remember Musa in the Book – surely he was sincere, and he was a Messenger, a Prophet.**
>
> **And We called to him from the right side of Mount Tur and drew him near to Us in intimate conversation.**
>
> **And in Our mercy We granted him his brother Harun, a Prophet. (19.51-53).**

And:

> **And We indeed gave Musa and Harun the means to discern (between right and wrong) and a light and a reminder for those who have *taqwa* – those who fear their Lord in secret and dread the Hour. (21.48-49).**

And, after describing *sayyedina* Nuh and the Messengers who came after him, peace be on him and them:

> **And then We sent Musa and his brother Harun with Our signs and clear authority to Firaoun and his chiefs – but they were scornful, and they were a people who were arrogant.**
>
> **And they said, 'Are we to believe in two men like ourselves, when their people are our slaves?'**
>
> **And they rejected both of them, and so they became among those who are destroyed.**
>
> **And We indeed gave Musa the Book so that perhaps they might be guided. (23.45-49).**

And:

> **And then We gave Musa the Book – complete for whoever would do good, and explaining everything, and a guidance and a mercy, so that perhaps they would believe in the meeting with their Lord. (6.154).**

And:

> **And We indeed gave Musa the Book and appointed his brother Harun with him as his helper.**
>
> **And We said, 'Go to the people who have denied Our signs,' – and then We utterly destroyed them. (25.35-36).**

Since Firaoun was aware that it had been predicted that a Prophet would be born amongst the Tribe of Israel at a certain time – and that such a man would inevitably challenge his power and authority – he ordered that all the sons who were born to women of the Tribe of Israel during that time should be killed.

It was during the time of this slaughter that the mother of *sayyedina* Musa was inspired by Allah to place her newly born son in a basket and to let it float down the river Nile, in the hope that it would carry him to safety:

> **We relate some of the story of Musa and Firaoun to you, with the truth, for people who believe:**
>
> **Surely Firaoun exalted himself in the land and made its people castes, a tribe of whom he oppressed, killing their sons and sparing their women – surely he was one of those who corrupt.**
>
> **And We desired to be kind to those who were oppressed in the land, and to make them leaders, and to make them the inheritors, and to strengthen them in the land, and to show Firaoun and Haman and their forces what they feared from them.**
>
> **And We inspired in the mother of Musa, (saying), 'Suckle him, and when you fear for him, then cast him into the river, and do not be afraid and do not be sad – surely We will bring him back to you and We will make him one of the Messengers.'**
>
> **And so the family of Firaoun looked after him, so that he would become an adversary and a cause of sorrow for them – surely Firaoun and Haman and their forces were always doing wrong.**
>
> **And the wife of Firaoun said, '(He will be) a joy to the eye for me and for you; do not kill him; perhaps he will be of use to us, or we can take him as a son,' – and they did not see.**
>
> **And the heart of Musa's mother became distraught. She would have given him away if We had not strengthened her heart so that she would be one of those who have faith.**
>
> **And she said to his sister, 'Follow him.' So she watched him at a distance – and they did not see.**

And We had already decreed that he could not have a foster-mother, so she said, 'Shall I show you a family who can bring him up for you and look after him well?'

So We restored him to his mother to be a joy to her eye and so that she would not grieve and so that she would know that the promise of Allah is true – but most of them do not know.

And when he reached his full strength and maturity We gave him wisdom and knowledge – and that is how We reward the good.

And he entered the city at a time when its people were careless, and in it he came across two men fighting, one from his own people, and the other from his enemies; and the one from his own people asked him for help against the one from his enemies – so Musa struck him with his fist and killed him. He said, 'This is *shaytan's* doing – surely he is an enemy, clearly one who misleads.'

He said, 'My lord, surely I have wronged myself, so forgive me,' and so He forgave him. Surely He is the Forgiving, the Compassionate.

He said, 'My lord, as You have blessed me, I will never be a help to the guilty again.'

And morning found him in the city, fearful, watchful – when the one who had asked him for help the day before cried out to him for help again.

Musa said to him, 'Surely you are indeed a fool!' And when he was about to attack the man who was an enemy to them both, he said, 'O Musa, are you going to kill me just as you killed someone yesterday? Do you want to be nothing but a tyrant in this land – and do you not want to be one of those who put things right?'

**And a man came running from the furthest part of the city, saying, 'O Musa, surely the leaders are planning to kill you, so go! – surely I am one of those who give you good advice.'**

**So he left there, fearful, watchful. He said, 'My lord, save me from the people who do wrong.'**

**And when he turned his face towards Midian, he said, 'Perhaps my lord will lead me along the right way.'**

**And when he reached the wells of Midian, he found a group of men there watering (their flocks), and he found two women holding back apart from them. He said, 'What is the matter with you?'**

**The two replied, 'We can not use the wells until the shepherds have finished – and our father is a very old man.'**

**So he drew water for them and then withdrew into the shade, and he said, 'My lord, surely I am in need of whatever good You may send.'**

(It is said that when *sayyedina* Musa first reached the wells at Midian, he was so emaciated that green vegetables could be seen in his stomach.)

**Then one of the two women approached him, walking shyly, and she said, 'Surely my father is asking for you, so that he can repay you for drawing water for us.'**

**And when he came to him, and told him his story, he said, 'Do not be afraid – you have escaped from the wrongdoers.'**

**One of the two women said, 'O my father, hire him; surely the best man to hire is the one who is strong, trustworthy.'**

**He said, 'Surely I would like to marry you to one of these two daughters of mine provided that you hire yourself to me for (a term of) eight pilgrimages; and if you complete**

**ten, then it is up to you, for I do not want to make it difficult for you. *Insh'Allah* you will find that I am one of the righteous.'**

**He replied, 'So let it be between you and me. Whichever of the two terms I fulfil, there will be no injustice to me – and Allah is witness to what we say.'** (28.3-28)

*Sayyedina* Musa accordingly married one of the old man's daughters, and remained in Midian for the agreed period of time. It is said that the father of Musa's wife was *sayyedina* Shu'aib, who – as we have already seen – was descended from *sayyedina* Ibrahim through Madyan, but not through Isma'il or Ishaq, peace be on all of them. When *sayyedina* Musa had completed his term in Midian, he left with his family, and it was then that he was made aware of his prophethood:

**Then, when Musa had fulfilled the term, and was travelling with his family, he saw a fire on the side of MountTur. He said to his family, 'Stay here – I have seen a fire – perhaps I may bring you news from there, or a brand from the fire, so that you can warm yourselves.'**

**And when he reached it, he was addressed from the right side of the valley, from the tree in the blessed place: 'O Musa, surely I, even I, am Allah, the Lord of the worlds. So throw down your staff!' – And when he saw it moving like a snake, he turned to flee and did not come back. – 'O Musa, draw near and do not be afraid; surely you are one of those who are safe. Put your hand into the neck of your robe – it will come out white without any harm – and keep yourself firm from fear. And these will be two proofs from your Lord to Firaoun and his chiefs; surely they are a wicked people.'**

**He replied, 'My lord, surely I killed one of them and I fear that they will kill me. And my brother Harun, he is more eloquent than I am in speech, so send him with me as a helper to confirm me – surely I fear that they will reject me.'**

He said, 'We will strengthen your arm with your brother, and We will give both of you power so that they cannot harm either of you – by Our signs, both you and whoever follows the two of you will be the winners.'

But when Musa came to them with Our clear signs, they said, 'This is nothing but false magic, and we never heard of this from our forefathers.'

And Musa said, 'My Lord knows best about who comes with guidance from His presence, and whose end will be the abode (of the Garden). Surely the wrong-doers will not be successful.'

And Firaoun said, 'O chiefs, I do not know of your having any god other than me, so kindle (a fire), O Haman, to bake the clay, and make me a high tower so that I can look down on the God of Musa – and indeed I certainly think he is one of the liars.'

And he and his forces were arrogant in the land without any justification, and they thought that they would never be brought back to Us. So We seized him and his forces, and We threw them in the sea – so see what happened to the wrong-doers!

And We made them a people who invite to the Fire, and on the Day of Standing they will not be helped.

And We made a curse follow them in this world, and on the Day of Standing they will be among those who are hated.

And We certainly gave the Book to Musa after We had destroyed the earlier generations – examples for mankind – and a guidance and a mercy so that perhaps they might remember.

And you were not on the western side (of Mount Tur) when We revealed the Law to Musa, and you were not among those who witnessed it.

**But We brought forth generations, and their lives lasted long. And you were not a dweller among the people of Midian, reciting Our signs to them, but We continued sending Messengers.**

**And you were not on the side of Mount Tur when We called, but it is a mercy from your Lord, so that you can warn a people to whom no warner came before, so that perhaps they may remember – and lest a disaster should afflict them because of what they had done with their own hands before so that they might say, 'Our Lord, if only You had sent a Messenger to us, then we would have followed Your signs, and we would have been among the believers.'**

**But when the truth came to them from Our presence, they said, 'If only he had been given the same as what was given to Musa.'**

**And did they not reject what was given to Musa before? They said, 'Two magics that support each other,' and they said, 'Surely we are disbelievers in both.' (28.29-48).**

Different aspects of *sayyedina* Musa's life are also related in greater detail or with greater emphasis in many other parts of the Qur'an. Thus, for example, the point at which *sayyedina* Musa was first informed of his prophethood – as well as what subsequently occurred – is also described in Surat An-Naml:

**(Remember) when Musa said to his family, 'I have seen a fire – I will bring you news from there, or I may bring you a burning brand so that you can warm yourselves.'**

**And when he reached it, he was addressed thus: 'Blessed is Whoever is in the fire and Whoever surrounds it and glory to Allah the Lord of the worlds. O Musa, surely I am Allah, the Mighty, the Wise. – And throw down your staff!'**

**And when he saw it moving like a snake, he turned to flee and did not come back. – 'O Musa, do not be afraid; surely Messengers are not afraid in My presence, except whoever**

**has done wrong and then turned to good after evil – and surely I am Forgiving, Compassionate.**

**'And put your hand into the neck of your robe – it will come out white without any harm. These are among nine signs for Firaoun and his people – surely they are a wicked people.'**

**But when Our signs came to them, plain to see, they said, 'This is clearly magic,' and they denied them, out of darkness and arrogance, even though their selves realised what they were – so see what the outcome was for those who were corrupt! (27.7-14).**

The point at which *sayyedina* Musa was first informed of his prophethood – as well as what subsequently occurred – is also described in Surah Ta-Ha:

**And has the story of Musa come to you? – When he saw a fire and said to his family, 'Stay here – I have seen a fire – perhaps I may bring you a light from there, or find guidance at the fire.'**

**And when he reached it, he was told, 'O Musa, surely I, even I, am your Lord, so take off your shoes – surely you are in the sacred valley of Tuwa. And I have chosen you, so listen to what is revealed:**

**'Surely I, even I, am Allah – there is no god but Me, so worship Me and establish the prayer in remembrance of Me.**

**'Surely the Hour is approaching, but I intend to keep it hidden, so that every self may be rewarded for what it strives for – so do not let whoever does not believe in it and follows his own desires turn you away from it so that you are destroyed.**

**'And what is that in your right hand, O Musa?'**

He replied, 'This is my staff on which I lean, and with which I beat down leaves for my sheep, and for which I find other uses.'

He said, 'Throw it down, O Musa!'

So he threw it down – and it became a writhing snake!

He said, 'Take hold of it and do not be afraid – We shall restore it to its former shape. And put your hand under your arm – it will come out white without any harm – another sign, so that We may show you some of Our greater signs.

'Go to Firaoun – surely he has exceeded the bounds.'

He replied, 'My Lord, ease my heart, and make my task easy for me, and free the impediment from my speech, so that they understand what I say, and appoint a helper from my family for me – Harun, my brother – increase my strength through him, and may he share in my task, so that we may glorify You a great deal and remember You a great deal – surely You are always watching us.'

He said, 'Your request is certainly granted, O Musa – and indeed We favoured you at another time, when We inspired what was inspired in your mother to, "Put him into the ark, and put it into the river, and the river will take it to the bank, and he will be taken by an enemy to Me and an enemy to him."

'And I protected you with love from Me so that you would be brought up in My sight – when your sister went and said, "Shall I show you someone who can nurse him?" So We returned you to your mother to be a joy to her eye and so that she would not grieve.

'And you killed someone, so We saved you from affliction and We tested you with trials – so you remained for years with the people of Madyan. Then you came (here) by decree, O Musa.

'And I have raised you for Myself.

'Go, you and your brother, with My signs and do not be lazy in remembering Me. Go, both of you, to Firaoun – surely he has exceeded the bounds. So speak to him with gentle words, so that perhaps he will be reminded or feel fear.'

They replied, 'Our Lord, surely we are afraid that he will be haughty with us, or that he will behave like a tyrant.'

He said, 'Do not be afraid – surely I am with you both, Hearing and Seeing – so go to him and say, "Surely we are two Messengers of your Lord, so send the Tribe of Israel with us, and do not afflict them. We have indeed come to you with a sign from our Lord – and peace will be for whoever follows the guidance. Surely it has indeed been revealed to us that affliction is for whoever rejects and turns away."'

He (Firaoun) said, 'And who is the Lord of you two, O Musa?'

He replied, 'Our Lord is the One Who gave every thing its natural form and then guided it.'

He said, 'So what is the condition of the earlier generations?'

He replied, 'The knowledge of that is with my Lord in a Book. My Lord does not make a mistake and He does not forget – the One Who has made the earth wide for you, and has made paths in it for you to walk along, and has made water fall from the sky,' – and from it We have brought forth different kinds of plants, (saying), 'Eat and pasture your cattle.' Surely in that there are signs for people who think. From it We have created you, and to it We shall return you, and from it We shall bring you forth a second time.

And We certainly showed him all of Our signs – but he denied and refused.

He said, 'Have you come to us to drive us out from our land with your magic, O Musa? Then we can surely bring you a magic like it – so choose a time which is agreed between us and between you, and which neither we nor you will miss, at a place which is mutually convenient.'

He replied, 'The meeting with you shall be on the day of the festival – and let the people gather at mid-morning.'

So Firaoun went away, and prepared his stratagem, and then came back.

Musa said to them, 'Woe to you! Do not invent a falsehood about Allah, lest He destroys you with an affliction – and whoever lies is certainly hopeless.'

So they debated with each other about what they should do, and kept their plan secret.

They said, 'Surely these two are certainly magicians who want to drive you out of your land with their magic and destroy your best traditions – so prepare your stratagem and then line up in ranks – and whoever wins today will indeed be successful.'

They said, 'O Musa, will you throw – or should we be the first to throw?'

He replied, 'No, you throw!' And then, by their magic, their ropes and their staffs appeared to be moving – and Musa began to feel afraid in himself.

We said, 'Do not be afraid – surely you will be higher. Throw what is in your right hand – it will swallow up what they have contrived. Surely what they have contrived is a magician's trick – and a magician will not be successful whatever he does.'

So the magicians threw themselves down prostrating – they said, 'We believe in the Lord of Harun and Musa.'

He (Firaoun) said, 'Do you put your faith in him before I have given you permission? Surely he must be your master who has taught you the magic. So surely I will cut off your hands and feet on opposite sides, and surely I will crucify you on the trunks of palm trees – and you will know for certain which of us has harsher and more lasting punishment.'

They said, 'We will never prefer you above the clear proofs which have come to us – and the One Who created us. So decree whatever you decree – surely your decree can only affect the life of this world. Surely we believe in our Lord – that He will forgive us our sins and the magic which you made us practise. And Allah is better and more lasting.'

Surely whoever comes to his Lord guilty, surely for him is Hell, in which he will neither die nor live.

And whoever comes to his Lord a believer, having done good, then for these are the high stations – Gardens of Eden underneath which rivers flow, living there for ever – and this is a reward for whoever purifies himself.

And We certainly inspired Musa to, 'Leave with My slaves, and then strike a dry path for them through the sea, without being afraid of being overtaken, or having any fear.'

And Firaoun followed them with his forces, and then the sea utterly overwhelmed them.

And Firaoun led his people astray – and he did not guide them.

O Tribe of Israel, We indeed delivered you from your enemy, and We made a covenant with you on the right side of Mount Tur, and We sent down manna and quails for you, (saying), 'Eat of the good things which We have provided

**for you, and do not be excessive in this, lest My anger descends on you – and whoever has My anger descend on him will certainly perish.**

**'And surely I am indeed Forgiving towards whoever turns in repentance, and believes, and does good, and then goes straight.'** (20.9-82).

While *sayyedina* Musa was receiving revelation from Allah on Mount Tur, peace be on him, the faith of the Tribe of Israel was tested in his absence:

**And (it was said to him), 'What has made you hurry away from your people, O Musa?'**

**He replied, 'They are close behind me – and I was hurrying to You, my Lord, to please You.'**

**He said, 'And surely we have tested your people in your absence – and As-Samiri has led them astray.'**

**So Musa returned to his people, angry and sad. He said, 'O my people, did not your Lord promise you a good promise? Did the time seem too long for you, or did you want the anger of your Lord to descend on you because you betrayed my trust?'**

**They replied, 'We did not mean to betray your trust, but we were burdened down with the weight of the people's ornaments, so we melted them down, which is what As-Samiri suggested.'**

**Then he made the form of a calf which lowed for them, so they said, 'This is your god, and the god of Musa – but he has forgotten.'**

**Did they not see that it did not speak back to them, and that it did not have the power to either harm or benefit them?**

**And Harun had indeed said to them before, 'O people, surely you are being tested with it, and surely your Lord is the Merciful, so follow me and obey my command.'**

**They said, 'We will not stop being devoted to it until Musa returns to us.'**

**He (Musa) said, 'O Harun, what stopped you, when you saw them going astray, that you did not obey me? Have you rebelled against my authority?'**

**He replied, 'O son of my mother, do not grasp me by my beard or by my head! Surely I was afraid lest you might say, "You have caused division among the Tribe of Israel, and did not wait for my decision."'**

**He (Musa) said, 'And what do you have to say, O Samiri?'**

**He replied, 'I saw what they did not see, so I picked up a handful of dust from the tracks of the Messenger [the angel Jibril] and then threw it into it [the mouth of the calf] – and that is what my self suggested to me.'**

**He said, 'Then go! And surely in this life it is for you to say, "Do not touch me!" And surely there is an appointed time for you which you cannot avoid. And look at your god to which you have continued to be devoted – we will certainly burn it and then completely scatter its ashes in the sea! Surely your God is Allah, the One other than Whom there is no god – except He. He encompasses all things in His knowledge.'**

**That is how We have told you some of the story of what happened long ago – and We have certainly given you a reminder from Our presence. (20.83-99).**

The reaction of Firaoun and his chiefs to the signs which Musa brought is also recorded in Surah Az-Zakhruf:

**And We indeed sent Musa with Our signs to Firaoun and his chiefs, and he said, 'Surely I am a Messenger of the Lord of the worlds', but when he brought them Our signs, they just laughed at them.**

**And We did not show them any sign which was not greater than the one before it, and We afflicted them with torment, so that they might turn back.**

**And they said, 'O magician, pray for us to your Lord, since He has a covenant with you – and surely we will certainly be rightly guided.'**

**But when We took away the torment from them, then they broke their word.**

**And Firaoun made a proclamation to his people, saying, 'O my people, does not the sovereignty over this city and these rivers which flow below me belong to me? Can you not see?**

**'Am I not better than this man who is common and cannot even speak clearly? – Then why have ornaments of gold not been sent down on him, and why have angels not been sent with him as companions?'**

**And so he made his people treat (Musa) lightly, and so they obeyed him – surely they were a wicked people.**

**And so when they angered Us, We paid them back, and so We drowned them all together.**

**And so We made history of them – and a lesson for those who came after. (43.46-56).**

The initial confrontation between *sayyedina* Musa and Firaoun, and then what subsequently occurred, is also described in Surat al-'Araf. After describing what happened to the people who rejected the earlier Prophets – the people of the townships – Allah says:

Then, after them, We sent Musa with Our signs to Firaoun and his chiefs, but they rejected them – so see what the outcome was for those who are corrupt:

And Musa said, 'O Firaoun, surely I am a Messenger from the Lord of the worlds, confirmed as such provided that I do not say anything about Allah except the truth. I have indeed come to you with a clear sign from your Lord, so let the Tribe of Israel go with me.'

He replied, 'If you have come with a sign, then show it, if you are one of those who are truthful.'

Then he threw down his staff – and it clearly became a snake.

And he drew out his hand (from under his arm) – and it became white for those who were watching.

The chiefs of Firaoun's people said, 'Surely this man is a clever magician who wishes to drive you out from your land, so what do you command?'

They said, 'Keep him and his brother waiting, and send summoners into the cities to bring every clever magician to you.'

And the magicians who came to Firaoun said, 'Surely we must have a reward if we are the winners.'

He replied, 'Yes – and surely you will indeed be among those who are near (to me).'

They said, 'O Musa, will you throw – or shall we be the ones to throw?'

He said, 'Throw!' – And when they threw, they mesmerised the eyes of the people, and filled them with awe, and contrived a mighty spell.

And We inspired in Musa to, 'Throw down your staff!' – And so it swallowed up the illusion which they had created.

And so the truth was made evident – and what they were doing was shown to be false.

And so they were overcome there, and brought low.

And the magicians fell down prostrating – they said, 'We believe in the Lord of the worlds, the Lord of Musa and Harun.'

Firaoun said, 'Do you believe in him before I have given you permission? Surely this is a plot which you have planned in the city to drive out its people from it. But you will come to know! Surely I will have your hands and your feet cut off on opposite sides, and then I will surely crucify you all together.'

They replied, 'Surely to our Lord we shall return. And are you only taking revenge on us because we have believed in the signs of our Lord when they came to us? Our Lord, pour out patience on us and let us die as Muslims.'

And the chiefs of Firaoun's people said (to Firaoun), 'Are you going to allow Musa and his people to create mischief in the land and forsake you and your gods?'

He replied, 'We will kill their sons and spare their women – and surely we will subdue them.'

Musa said to his people, 'Seek help in Allah and be patient. Surely the earth belongs to Allah – He bequeaths it to whomever of his slaves He wishes, and the outcome is for those who have *taqwa*.

They replied, 'We have suffered harm before you came to us and since you came to us.'

He said, 'It may be that your Lord will destroy your enemy and make you *khalifs* in the earth, so that He can see how you behave.'

And We certainly afflicted the people of Firaoun with famine and failed crops so that perhaps they might take heed – but whenever good came to them, they said, 'This is because of us,' and whenever evil afflicted them, they attributed it to Musa and whoever was with him – when in fact what they were interpreting was from Allah, but most of them did not realise.

And they said, 'Whatever sign you may bring to bewitch us with, we will never believe you.'

So We sent the flood, and the locusts, and the lice, and the frogs, and the blood, against them – obvious signs – but they were arrogant and they were a sinful people.

And when the plague overwhelmed them, they said, 'O Musa, pray for us to your Lord, since He has a covenant with you – and if you take away the plague from us, we will certainly believe in you, and we will certainly let the Tribe of Israel go with you.'

But when We took the plague away from them for a certain time for them to do so, they broke their promise.

And so We took revenge on them and drowned them in the sea, because they rejected Our signs and did not pay attention to them.

And We made the people who had been weak inherit the east and the west of the land which We had blessed; and the good word of your Lord was fulfilled for the Tribe of Israel because of their patience; and We destroyed what Firaoun and his people had been doing and what they had established.

And We brought the Tribe of Israel across the sea, and they came across a people who were devoted to their idols.

They (the Tribe of Israel) said, 'O Musa, make a god for us like the gods which they have.'

He replied, 'Surely you are an ignorant people! As for them, surely what they have will be utterly destroyed, and what they are doing is false.'

He said, 'How could I want a god for you other than Allah – when He has favoured you the most in all the worlds?'

And (remember) when We delivered you from the people of Firaoun while they were inflicting a dreadful affliction on you, killing your sons and sparing your women? – And in that was a tremendous trial from your Lord.

And We appointed thirty nights for Musa, and added another ten to them – and so he completed the time appointed by his Lord of forty nights – and Musa said to his brother Harun, 'Stand in for me over my people, and do right, and do not follow the way of those who make mischief.'

And when Musa came to keep the appointment which We had made, and his Lord had spoken to him, he said, 'My Lord, show (Yourself) to me so that I can look at You.'

He replied, 'You can not see Me – but look at the mountain, and if it remains standing in its place, then you will see Me.'

And when his Lord revealed His majesty to the mountain, He reduced it to dust, and Musa fell down as if struck by lightning. And when he came to his senses, he said, 'Glory be to You – I turn to You in repentance, and I am the first of the believers!'

He said, 'O Musa, surely I have chosen you above all people by My messages and by My speaking (to you), so hold to

**what I have given you, and be one of those who are thankful.'**

**And We inscribed for him on the tablets commands for everything and an explanation of everything, and (told him), 'Hold to it firmly and command your people, "Hold to the best of it."'**

**I shall show you the abode of those who are wicked. I shall turn away from My signs those who are arrogant in the land without any justification – and even if they see every sign they will not believe in it, and even if they see the right way they will not take that way, and if they see the wrong way they will take that way. That is because they deny Our signs and are used to disregarding them.**

**And the actions of those who deny Our signs and the meeting in the next world are fruitless. Are they rewarded for anything other than what they used to do?**

**And in his absence, the people of Musa chose a calf made from their ornaments which made a lowing sound. Did they not see that it could not speak to them, nor guide them on any way – they chose it and became wrong doers.**

**And when they regretted what they had done and realised that they had indeed gone astray, they said, 'Unless our Lord has mercy on us, and forgives us, we will certainly be among the losers.'**

**And when Musa returned to his people, angered and saddened, he said, 'What you have done in my absence is evil. Do you wish to bring about the command of your Lord?'**

**And he threw down the tablets, and took hold of his brother by the head, dragging him towards himself.**

**He (Harun) said, 'Son of my mother, surely the people considered me weak and nearly killed me – so do not make my**

**enemies laugh at me, and do not include me among the wrong doers!'**

**He (Musa) said, 'My Lord, forgive me and my brother and bringus into Your mercy – and You are the most merciful of those who are merciful.'**

**Surely those who chose the calf will experience anger from their Lord and humiliation in the life of this world – and that is how We reward those who are liars.**

**And those who do evil deeds and then after that turn in repentance and believe – surely after that your Lord is indeed Forgiving, Compassionate.**

**And when Musa's anger had calmed down, he picked up the tablets – and in what was inscribed on them was guidance and mercy for all those who fear their Lord.**

**And Musa chose seventy men from his people for an appointed time with Us – and when they started trembling, he said, 'My Lord, if You had wanted, you could have already destroyed them and me. Are You going to destroy us because of what the foolish ones among us have done? It is nothing but a test from You – by it You send astray whomever You wish and You guide whomever You wish. You are our protecting friend, so forgive us and have mercy on us – and You are the best of those who forgive. And decree what is good for us in this life and in the next life – surely we have turned to You.'**

**He replied, 'I inflict My punishment on whomever I wish – and My mercy encompasses everything, so I shall decree it for those who have *taqwa* and pay the *zakat*, and those who believe in Our signs.' (7.103-156).**

There is also a reference to the confrontation between *sayyedina* Musa and Firaoun and his magicians in Surah Ash-Shu'ara:

And (remember) when your Lord told Musa to, 'Go to the people who are wrong doers, the people of Firaoun! Will they not have *taqwa*?'

He replied, 'My Lord, surely I am afraid that they will deny me, and my heart will feel constricted, and I will not be able to speak clearly – so send Harun with me.

'And they have a crime against me – and so I am afraid that they will kill me.'

He replied, 'No indeed! Go, both of you, with Our signs – surely We will be with you, listening – so go to Firaoun and say, "Surely we bring a message from the Lord of the worlds, to let the Tribe of Israel go with us."'

He (Firaoun) replied, 'Did we not bring you up among us as a child, and then you remained with us for many years of your life, and then you did the deed which you did – and (now) you are one of those who reject (us)?'

He (Musa) said, 'I did that then, when I was one of those who are astray, so I fled from you because I was afraid of you, and then my Lord granted me wisdom and made me one of the Messengers – and that favour with which you reproach me (now) was only as a result of your having enslaved the Tribe of Israel.'

Firaoun replied, 'And who is the Lord of the worlds?'

He said, 'The Lord of the heavens and the earth and whatever is between them, if you really want to know.'

He (Firaoun) said to those around him. 'Did you hear that?'

He said, 'Your Lord and the Lord of your forefathers!'

He replied, 'Surely your Messenger who has been sent to you is certainly a madman!'

He said, 'Lord of the East and the West and whatever is between them, if you could only understand.'

He replied, 'If you choose any god other than me, I will certainly put you with those who are in prison!'

He said, 'Even if I show you something clear?'

He replied, 'Show it then, if you are one of those who are truthful.'

So he threw down his staff and it clearly became a snake.

And he drew out his hand (from under his arm) – and it became white for those who were watching.

He (Firaoun) said to the chiefs around him, 'Surely this man is a clever magician who wishes to drive you out from your land with his magic, so what do you command?'

They said, 'Keep him and his brother waiting, and send summoners into the cities to bring every clever magician to you.'

So the magicians gathered together at the right time on the day which had been appointed.

And it was said to the people, 'Will you gather together too – so that we can follow the magicians if they are the winners?'

And when the magicians came, they said to Firaoun, 'Will there surely be a reward for us if we are the winners?'

He replied, 'Yes – and surely you will then certainly be among those who are near (to me).'

Musa said to them, 'Throw what you are going to throw!'

So they threw down their ropes and their staffs, and they said, 'By the might of Firaoun surely we are certainly the winners!'

And then Musa threw down his staff – and it swallowed up the illusion which they had created.

And the magicians fell down prostrating – they said, 'We believe in the Lord of the worlds, the Lord of Musa and Harun.'

(Firaoun) said, 'Do you believe in him before I have given you permission? Surely he must be your master who has taught you the magic – but you will certainly come to know! Surely I will cut off your hands and feet on opposite sides, and surely I will crucify you all together.'

They replied, 'It will do no harm – surely we shall return to our Lord; surely we hope that our Lord will forgive us our sins because we are the first to be believers.'

And We inspired Musa to, 'Go with My slaves by night, for surely you will be pursued.'

So Firaoun sent summoners into the cities, (who said), 'Surely these are only a small group, and surely they have certainly provoked us, and surely we are a host to be feared.'

So We led them away from (their) gardens and springs and treasures and fine dwellings – just like that – and We made the Tribe of Israel inherit them.

And they caught up with them at sunrise, and when the two hosts saw each other, the companions of Musa said, 'Surely we are certainly trapped!'

He replied, 'Certainly not! Surely my Lord is with me – He will guide me.'

**And We inspired Musa to, 'Strike the sea with your staff!' and it parted, and each part was like a huge mountain.**

**And then we brought the others in close behind, and We saved Musa and whoever was with him all together, and then We drowned the others.**

**Surely in that there is certainly a sign – and yet most of them are not believers.**

**And surely your Lord – He is certainly the Mighty, the Compassionate. (26.10-68).**

There is also a reference to the confrontation between *sayyedina* Musa and Firaoun and his magicians in Surah Yunus. After referring to *sayyedina* Nuh and to the Messengers who came after him, peace be on him and them, Allah says:

**Then after them We sent Musa and Harun to Firaoun and his chiefs with Our signs, but they were arrogant, and they were a sinful people.**

**And when the truth came to them from Our presence, they said, 'Surely this is clearly magic!'**

**Musa said, 'Is this how you describe the truth when it comes to you? Is this magic? – and magicians do not succeed!'**

**They replied, 'Have you come to us to turn us away from what we found our fathers doing, so that you two can be great in the land? – We are not going to believe you two!'**

**And Firaoun said, 'Bring every clever magician to me.'**

**And when the magicians came, Musa said to them, 'Throw what you are going to throw!'**

**And when they had thrown, Musa said, 'What you have produced is magic. Surely Allah will destroy it! Surely Allah does not protect the work of those who do mischief.'**

And Allah will vindicate the truth by His words, however much the sinners may detest it.

And no one believed in Musa except some youths from his people who were afraid of Firaoun and their chiefs, lest he would persecute them – and surely Firaoun was certainly in authority in the land, and surely he was indeed one of those who exceed the limits.

And Musa said, 'O my people, if you have believed in Allah then put your trust in Him, if you are Muslims.'

And they said, 'In Allah we put our trust – our Lord, do not use us to test the people who are wrong doers, and in Your mercy deliver us from the people who reject.'

And We inspired Musa and his brother to, 'Prepare houses for your people in the city, and make your houses places of worship, and establish the prayer – and give good news to the believers!'

And Musa said, 'Our Lord, surely You have given Firaoun and his chiefs splendour and wealth in the life of this world, our Lord, so that they lead (people) away from Your way. Our Lord, destroy their wealth and harden their hearts so that they will not believe until they see the painful punishment!'

He replied, 'Your prayer has been answered, so go straight, and do not follow the way of those who do not know.'

And We brought the Tribe of Israel across the sea – and Firaoun and his forces pursued them eagerly and defiantly – until, when he was suddenly overwhelmed by the water, he said, 'I believe that there is surely no god except the One in Whom the Tribe of Israel believe – and I am one of the Muslims!'

What? Now? – When up to now you rebelled and were one of those who are corrupt? – So this day We will preserve

**your body so that you can be a sign for whoever comes after you. And surely most of mankind certainly pay no attention to Our signs.**

**And We indeed settled the Tribe of Israel in an excellent abode, and We provided them with good things – and they did not disagree until after knowledge came to them. Surely your Lord will judge between them as regards what they disagreed about on the Day of Standing.** (10.75-93).

Thus, as *sayyedina* Musa himself had pointed out to Firaoun earlier on, the Pharaoh's belated profession of belief in Allah at the point of death was the last minute expression of what he had always known deep within himself but stubbornly refused to admit:

**And We indeed gave Musa nine clear signs – just ask the Tribe of Israel how he came to them and Firaoun said to him, 'Surely I think, O Musa, that you are bewitched!'**

**He replied, 'You know very well that these (signs) have not been sent down by anyone except the Lord of the heavens and the earth as clear proofs – and surely I certainly think, O Firaoun, that you are lost!'**

**And he wished to force them out from the land, but We drowned him and whomever was with him all together.**

**And We said to the Tribe of Israel, after him, 'Dwell in the land – but when the time for the next world comes, We shall gather you together in a mixed crowd.'** (17.101-104).

It is interesting to note in passing that historical and scientific research has established that the body of the Pharaoh who was drowned while pursuing *sayyedina* Musa and the Tribe of Israel has indeed been preserved as a sign for mankind up to this day. In his book, *The Bible, the Qur'an, and Science,* Maurice Bucaille concludes that the Pharaoh who looked after *sayyedina* Musa in his infancy was Ramesses II, that Ramesses II subsequently died while *sayyedina* Musa was in Midian, and that the son of Ramesses II, who was called Merneptah, was the Pharaoh who rejected *sayyedina* Musa's invitation to worship Allah and who was drowned in the Red sea.

The radiographic and endoscopic examinations which were carried out in 1975 on the mummified body of Merneptah (which had been discovered by Loret at Thebes in the Valley of the Kings in 1898) revealed, in Bucaille's words, 'multiple lesions of the bones with broad lacunae, some of which may have been mortal ... He most probably died either from drowning, according to the Scriptural narrations, or from very violent shocks preceding the moment when he was drowned – or both at once.'

The ultimate fate of the Pharaoh who was drowned in the Red sea is described in the following passage from Surah Hud:

> **And We indeed sent Musa with Our signs and clear authority to Firaoun and his chiefs, but they followed Firaoun's command – and the command of Firaoun was not the right way.**
>
> **He will go ahead of his people on the Day of Standing, and he will lead them down into the Fire – and how awful the place down to which they are led!**
>
> **And they are followed by a curse in this life and on the Day of Standing – how awful the gift which they will be given! (11.96-99).**

The ultimate fate of the Pharaoh who rejected *sayyedina* Musa is also described in greater detail in Surat al-Mumin, in a passage which also tells of one of the Pharoah's family who secretly believed in Allah and His Messenger, *sayyedina* Musa:

> **And We indeed sent Musa with Our signs and clear authority to Firaoun and Haman and Qarun, but they said, 'A false magician!'**
>
> **And when he came to them with the truth from Our presence, they said, 'Kill the sons of those who believe with**

him, and spare their women,' – but the stratagem of the disbelievers is never anything but misguided.

And Firaoun said, 'Let me kill Musa – and let him call on his Lord! Surely I fear that he will change your way of life, or that he will spread corruption in the land.'

And Musa said, 'Surely I seek refuge in My Lord and your Lord from every arrogant person who does not believe in the Day of Reckoning.'

And a man from the family of Firaoun who was a believer – but who concealed his belief – said, 'Are you going to kill a man because he says, "My Lord is Allah," and who has indeed come to you with clear proofs from your Lord?

'And if he is telling you lies, then his lying is against himself – and if he is telling you the truth, then some of what he has warned you about will happen to you. Surely Allah does not guide whoever is excessive and deceitful.

'O my people, the kingdom is yours today – you are dominant in the land – but who would save us from the wrath of Allah if it came upon us?'

Firaoun said, 'I am only letting you know what I know, and I am only guiding you to the right way.'

And the man who believed said, 'O my people, surely I fear you will share the same fate as those who rebelled (before you) – as with what happened to the people of Nuh, and A'ad, and Thamud, and those who came after them – and Allah never wishes to be unjust to His slaves.

'And O my people, surely I fear for you a Day when you are summoned, a Day when you will turn to flee because there is no one to save you from Allah – and whomever Allah leads astray, there is no guide for him.

'And Yusuf indeed came to you in the past with clear proofs, butyou did not stop doubting what he had brought you until, when he died, you said, "Allah will not send another Messenger after him."

'That is how Allah leads astray whoever is excessive and sceptical, those who argue about the signs of Allah without their being given any authority. This is very hateful to Allah and to those who believe. That is how Allah seals every arrogant, tyrannical heart.'

And Firaoun said, 'O Haman, build a tower for me so that I can reach the ways, the ways of heaven, and look down upon the God of Musa – and surely I think that he is certainly a liar!'

And that is how the evil of his actions was made to seem pleasing to Firaoun, and he was turned away from the right way, and the stratagem of Firaoun only ended in disaster.

And the man who believed said, 'O my people, follow me – I will guide you to the right way.

'O my people, surely the life of this world is a pastime – and surely the next life is the abode that lasts.

'Whoever does something evil will only be rewarded with something like it, and whoever does good – whether a man or a woman who is a believer – then they will enter the Garden, in which they will be provided for without any reckoning.

'And O my people, how is it that I am calling you to deliverance and you are calling me to the Fire! – You are calling me to reject Allah and to associate what I do not understand as a partner with Him, and I am calling you to the Mighty, the Forgiving.

'There is no doubt that what you are calling me to will surely have no influence in this world or in the next world, and that our return will be to Allah, and that those who exceeded the limits will be the companions of the Fire.

'And you will remember what I am saying to you, and I entrust my affair to Allah – surely Allah watches over His slaves!'

So Allah protected him from the evils which they planned and a terrible punishment overwhelmed the people of Firaoun – the Fire, to which they are exposed in the morning and in the evening. And on the Day when the Hour has come (it will be said), 'Lead the people of Firaoun to the most intense torment!'

And when they are wrangling in the Fire, then the weak will say to those who were arrogant, 'Surely we were following you, so can you relieve us from part of the Fire?'

Those who were arrogant will reply, 'Surely we are all in it together – surely Allah has already passed judgement on (His) slaves.'

And those who are in the Fire will say to the keepers of Hell, 'Ask your Lord to alleviate the torment for us for a day.'

They will reply, 'Did not your Messengers come to you with clear proofs?'

They will say, 'Yes, certainly.'

They will reply, 'Then you ask – although the prayer of those who reject is always in vain.'

Surely We will certainly help Our Messengers and those who believe, in the life of this world and on a Day when the witnesses stand firm – a Day when their excuses will not do the wrong doers any good, and when the curse is on them, and when the evil abode is theirs.

**And We indeed gave Musa the guidance, and We made the Tribe of Israel inherit the Book, a guidance and a reminder for people who understand. (40.23-54).**

It should be noted in passing that the wife of the Pharaoh who looked after *sayyedina* Musa when he was a child – whose name was Asiyya – was also a believer, in spite of her husband's deep arrogance and disbelief:

**And Allah has struck a metaphor of those who believe: the wife of Firaoun, when she said, 'My Lord, prepare a home for me with You in the Garden, and deliver me from Firaoun and his actions, and deliver me from people who are wrong doers. (66.11).**

It should also be noted in passing that Haman and Qarun, who are both mentioned at the beginning of the passage from Surat al-Mumin which has just been quoted, were two of Firaoun's richest and most influential chiefs. Indeed it was Qarun's immense wealth which ultimately contributed to his downfall:

**Surely Qarun was from the people of Musa, but he oppressed them. And We gave him so much treasure that even the keys for it were certainly a heavy burden for a company of strong men.**

**When his people said to him, 'Do not exult – surely Allah does not love those who exult – and, with what Allah has given you, seek the next world, and do not forget about your part in this world, and do good, just as Allah has been good to you, and do not seek corruption in the land – surely Allah does not love those who are corrupt,'**

**He replied, 'Surely I have only been given it because of the knowledge which I have.'**

**Did he not know that Allah had already destroyed generations of people before him who were mightier than him in power, and who had amassed more? – But the guilty ones will not be asked about their wrong actions.**

> And so he went out among his people in his splendour.
>
> Those who longed for the life of this world said, 'O if only we could have the same as what Qarun has been given! – surely he is very lucky indeed!'
>
> But those who had been given knowledge said, 'Woe to you! Allah's reward for whoever believes and does good is better – and no one will earn it except those who are patient.'
>
> And so We made the earth swallow him and his house up – and there was no one who could help him from Allah, and he was not one of those who can help themselves.
>
> And morning found those – who only the day before had been longing to be in his place – saying, 'Allah certainly increases provision for whomever of His slaves He wishes – and He decreases it. If Allah had not been generous to us, He would have made it swallow us up too! Those who reject certainly never prosper!'
>
> As for the abode of the next world, We give it to those who do not wish to be exalted in the land, or to be corrupt – and the outcome is for those who have *taqwa.*
>
> Whoever brings good will have better than it, and as for whoever brings evil – those who do evil things will only be treated in accordance with what they used to do. (28.76-84).

Haman and Qarun are also mentioned in Surat al-Ankabut, where after referring to some of the earlier Prophets and what happened to those who rejected them, Allah says:

> And (remember) Qarun and Firaoun and Haman – and Musa indeed came to them with clear proofs, but they were arrogant in the land – and they were not the winners.
>
> So we took each one in his wrong action – and of them there was the one on whom We sent a rain of stones; and of them there was the one who was taken by the blast; and of them

**there was the one whom We made the earth swallow up; and of them there was the one whom We drowned – and it was not that Allah was wronging them, but they were wronging themselves.**

**The metaphor of those who choose other guardians instead of Allah is the metaphor of the spider: it chooses its dwelling place – and surely the frailest of all dwelling places is certainly the dwelling place of the spider – if they only realised.**

**Surely Allah knows whatever thing they call on instead of Him – and He is the Mighty, the Wise.**

**And as for metaphors, We strike them for mankind – but no one grasps their meaning except those who have understanding. (29.39-43).**

The fate of Firaoun and his forces is also referred to in these *ayat*:

**And in Musa (there is also a sign) when We sent him to Firaoun with clear authority.**

**But he turned away with his chiefs and said, 'A magician, or a madman!'**

**So We seized him and his forces and We flung them into the sea – and he was to blame. (51.38-40).**

And:

**And warnings certainly came to the people of Firaoun, but they denied every one of Our signs, so We seized them with the grasp of the Mighty, the Powerful. (54.41-42).**

And:

**And Firaoun, and those who were before him, and the communities that were destroyed, were sinful.**

**And so they disobeyed the Messenger of their Lord, and so He punished them with an overwhelming punishment. (69.9-10).**

And:

**And We indeed tested Firaoun's people before them, when a noble Messenger came to them (telling them) to, 'Give back the slaves of Allah to me – surely I am a trustworthy messenger to you,' and, 'Do not be haughty towards Allah – surely I have come to you with clear authority, and surely I have sought refuge in my Lord and your Lord lest you should stone me, and if you do not believe in me, then leave me alone.'**

**And he called to his Lord (saying), 'These are a sinful people!'**

**So (he was told), 'Take away my slaves by night – surely you will be pursued – and then leave the sea behind you at your ease, for surely by then they will be an army that has been drowned.'**

**How many were the gardens and the springs that they left behind, and fields of grain and fine dwellings, and the pleasures in which they took delight – just like that – and We made another people inherit them.**

**And the heaven and the earth did not weep for them – and they were not reprieved.**

**And We indeed delivered the Tribe of Israel from humiliating affliction, from Firaoun – surely he was among the most extreme of those who exceed the limits.**

**And We indeed chose them, intentionally, above all the worlds, and We gave them signs in which there was clearly a trial.**

**And indeed these are the ones who are saying, 'It is that we only die once, and we will not be brought back to life again – so bring back our fathers if you are speaking truthfully!'**

**Are they better, or are the people of Tubb'a and those before them? We destroyed them, for surely they were sinful.**

('Tubb'a' was the title given to the kings of southern Arabia, just as every king of Egypt was called 'Firaoun'.)

**And We did not create the heavens and the earth and what is between them as a game.**

**We did not create them except with the Truth – but most of them do not know.**

**Surely the Day of Judgement is an appointed time for all of them – a Day on which a friend cannot be of any help to a friend – and they will not be helped, except on whomever Allah has mercy – surely He is the Mighty, the Compassionate. (44.17-42).**

There are many other references in various parts of the Qur'an to what happened to Musa and the Tribe of Israel after the Red sea had parted for them to allow them to cross safely over into Sinai before closing back over Firaoun and his forces and drowning them. The following *ayat* appear in Surat al-Baqarah:

**O Tribe of Israel, remember My blessing with which I blessed you, and how I favoured you the most in all the worlds, and be aware of a Day when no self will be of any good to another self, and intercession will not be accepted from it, and compensation will not be acceptable from it – and they will not be helped.**

**And (remember) when We delivered you from the people of Firaoun, who were inflicting a dreadful affliction on you, slaughtering your sons and sparing your women? – And in that was a tremendous trial from your Lord.**

**And when We parted the sea for you and rescued you – and drowned the people of Firaoun as you watched.**

**And when We appointed forty nights with Musa – and then you turned to the calf while he was absent and were wrong doers.**

**Then after that We forgave you, so that you might be grateful.**

**And when We gave Musa the Book and the means to discern (between right and wrong), so that you might be guided.**

**And when Musa said to his people, 'O my people, surely you have wronged yourselves by your turning to the calf, so turn in repentance to your Creator and overcome your selves – that will be best for you as regards your Creator and He will relent towards you – surely He is the Relenting, the Compassionate.'**

**And when you said, 'O Musa, we will not believe in you until we see Allah clearly,' – and the lightning struck you as you looked – and then We brought you back to life after you had been dead so that perhaps you might be thankful.**

**And We shaded you with clouds, and We sent down manna and quails for you, (saying), 'Eat of the good things with which We have provided you' – and they did not wrong Us, but they wronged themselves.**

**And when We said, 'Go into this town and eat as much as you want from what is in it – and enter the gate prostrating and saying, "Seeking forgiveness" – We will forgive you your wrong actions, and We will give more to those who do good.'**

**But those who did wrong changed the word to something other than what they had been told – so We sent down a punishment on those who did wrong from the sky because of their disobedience.**

And when Musa asked for water for his people, and We said, 'Strike the rock with your staff!' and twelve springs gushed out from it, so that each tribe knew their drinking place – 'Eat and drink of what Allah has provided, and do not do evil in the land, making mischief.'

And when you said, 'O Musa, we can not put up with one kind of food, so ask your Lord for us to give us what grows from the earth – its herbs, and its cucumbers, and its garlic, and its lentils, and its onions.'

He replied, 'Do you want to exchange what is better for what is worse? – Go down to a city, and you will surely have what you want.'

And they were stamped with humiliation and poverty, and they incurred the anger of Allah – that was because they rejected the signs of Allah and killed the Prophets without any justification. That was because they rebelled and were wicked.

Surely those who believe and those who are Jews and Christians and Sabaeans – whoever believes in Allah and the Last Day and does good – their reward is with their Lord, and they will not feel afraid and they will not be sad.

And (remember) when We made a covenant with you and made Mount Tur tower above you, (saying), 'Take a firm hold of what We have given to you, and remember what is in it, so that you may have *taqwa*.'

Then after that, you turned away – and if it had not been for the generosity of Allah towards you, and His mercy, you certainly would have been among the losers.

And you certainly know about those of you who broke the sabbath – so We said to them, 'Be stupid apes! And so We made an example of them for whoever was there and for whoever came after – and a warning to those who have *taqwa*.

And when Musa said to his people, 'Surely Allah has commanded you to sacrifice a cow,' they said, 'Are you making fun of us?'

He replied, 'I seek refuge in Allah from being among the ignorant!'

They said, 'Ask your Lord for us to make clear to us what (kind of cow) it should be.'

He replied, 'Surely He says that it should be a cow which is neither old nor young – half way between the two – so do as you have been told.'

They said, 'Ask your Lord for us to make clear to us what colour it should be.'

He replied, 'Surely He says that it should be a yellow cow, whose bright colour is pleasing to look at.'

They said, 'Ask your Lord for us to make clear to us what it should be (like) – surely cows seem all alike to us – and *insh'Allah* we will indeed be guided.'

He replied, 'Surely He says that it should be a cow which has not been broken in to plough the soil or water the fields – sound and without any flaw in her.'

They said, 'Now you have given an accurate description.' And so they sacrificed her – although they nearly did not do it.

And (remember) when you killed someone and then disagreed about (who had done) it – and Allah exposed what you were hiding.

And We said, 'Strike it with part of it!' – That is how Allah gives life to the dead and shows you His signs so that perhaps you may understand.'

(It is said that when it was hit with part of it, the person came alive, pointed at the murderer, and then died again.)

**Then after that your hearts hardened and became like stones, or even more intensely hard – for surely there are some stones from which rivers gush; and surely there are some from which, when they are split open, water pours; and surely there are some which fall down out of fear of Allah – and Allah is not unaware of what you do. (2.47-74).**

The incident in which the people of Musa were struck down dead – because they said they would not believe in Musa unless they saw Allah clearly – and were then brought back to life is also referred to in the following *ayah*:

**Have you not reflected on those who went out from their homes in their thousands, fearing death, and Allah said to them, 'Die!' and then He brought them back to life – surely Allah is certainly Lord of generosity towards mankind, but most people are not grateful. (2.243).**

It is clear from the following *ayat* from Surah Ibrahim that however the Tribe of Israel behaved – whether they were obedient and grateful to Allah, or not – this did not affect Allah in the least:

**And We indeed sent Musa with Our signs to, 'Lead your people out of darkness into light, and remind them of the days of Allah.' Surely in that there are certainly signs for everyone who is patient (and) thankful.**

**And (remember) when Musa said to his people, 'Remember Allah's blessing upon you, when He delivered you from the people of Firaoun, who were inflicting a dreadful affliction on you, and slaughtering your sons and sparing your women – and in that was a tremendous trial from your Lord.**

**'And when your Lord declared, "If you are thankful, I will certainly give you more, but if you are ungrateful, surely My punishment is intense."'**

**And Musa said, 'Even if you are ungrateful, you and all who are on the earth – then surely Allah is still All-Sufficient, Worthy of Praise!'** (14.5-8).

And just as Allah is never in any need of anything that He has created, so also He is always present:

**Has the story of the forces of Firaoun come to you – and of Thamud?**

**Yet those who reject persist in their denial – and Allah, hidden from their sight, surrounds them.** (85.17-20).

It was the Tribe of Israel's inability to hold firmly to the guidance which had been revealed to *sayyedina* Musa, combined with their tendency to ask too many questions when none were in fact needed, which resulted in a delay of forty years wandering aimlessly in the wilderness, before they were able to enter and settle in the holy land of Palestine which Allah had promised to them:

**And (remember) when Musa said to his people, 'O my people, remember Allah's blessing upon you, when He appointed Prophets from among you, and made you kings, and gave you what He had not given to anyone else in all the worlds. O my people, go into the Holy Land which Allah has written for you, and do not turn back on your heels – for then you would return as losers.'**

**They replied, 'O Musa, surely there are a powerful people there, and surely we will not go there until they have left it – so when they leave it, then we will go.'**

**Two of the men whom Allah had blessed, who feared (Him), said, 'Go through the gate against them, for if you go through it, then surely you will be victorious – and put your trust in Allah, if you are believers.'**

**They replied, 'O Musa, surely we will never go there while they are there – so go, you and your Lord, and fight! – surely we will stay here.'**

He said, 'My Lord, surely I do not have control over anyone except myself and my brother – so make a distinction between us and the people who are disobedient.'

He (Allah) replied, 'For this it shall remain closed to them for forty years, while they wander aimlessly in the land – so do not be saddened by the people who are disobedient.'

And tell them about the true story of the two sons of Adam (Kabil and Habil) – how they both offered a sacrifice, and it was accepted from one of them, but not accepted from the other, who said, 'I will certainly kill you!'

(The other) replied, 'Surely Allah only accepts (the actions) of those who have *taqwa*. Even if you raise your hand against me to kill me, I will not raise my hand to kill you – surely I fear Allah, the Lord of the worlds. Surely I would rather that you carry the blame for my sin and your sin and so become one of the people of the Fire – and that is the reward of those who do wrong.'

But (the other's) self insisted that he kill his brother, so he killed him – and so he became one of the losers.

Then Allah sent a raven who scratched at the ground in order to show him how to conceal the evil (he had done) to his brother.

He said, 'Woe is me – is it possible to be like this raven and so conceal the evil (I have done) to my brother?' – and so he became one of those who repent.

It is for that reason that We decreed for the Tribe of Israel that whoever kills someone for other than another life, or for spreading corruption in the earth, then surely it is as if he had killed all mankind, and that whoever saves a life, then it is as if he had saved all mankind. And Our Messengers certainly came to them with clear proofs, but after that many of them certainly exceeded the limits in the earth. (5.20-32).

The story of the Tribe of Israel is concisely summed up in this *ayah* from Surat as-Saff:

> **And (remember) when Musa said to his people, 'O my people, why do you persecute me when you well know that I am the Messenger of Allah to you?' So when they went astray Allah sent their hearts astray. And Allah does not guide the people who are evil. (61.5).**

It may have been during the period of forty years wandering in the wilderness – and it is not evident exactly when from the account given in the Qur'an – that there occurred the famous meeting between a man called Al-Khidr and *sayyedina* Musa, peace be on them, during which Allah made it clear that there are different kinds of knowledge and understanding and wisdom, and that He gives them to whom He wishes when He wishes.

It has been transmitted by Ibn 'Abbas, may Allah be pleased with him, that the Prophet Muhammad, may Allah bless him and grant him peace, said that one of the Tribe of Israel once asked *sayyedina* Musa if he knew of anyone who knew more than him. When *sayyedina* Musa said that he did not, Allah informed him that there was such a man, called Al-Khidr. *Sayyedina* Musa asked how he could meet him, and was told to take a fish with him when he went looking for him: wherever he lost the fish, which would be at the point where two seas meet, would be the place where he would find Al-Khidr. (Al-Bukhari).

The Qur'anic account of what happened is in Surat al-Kahf, and begins at the point where *sayyedina* Musa and a servant of his – who, according to the *hadith* transmitted by Ibn 'Abbas was Yusha' ibn Nun – are searching for the point where two seas meet:

> **And (remember) when Musa said to his servant, 'I will not give up until I reach the meeting of the two seas – even if I continue for ages.'**
>
> **And when they reached the point where the two meet, they forgot about their fish, which made its way straight into the waters.**

And when they had gone on further, he said to his servant, 'Bring us our meal – we have indeed found our journey tiring.'

He replied, 'Didn't you see, when we rested by the rock, and I forgot about the fish – and only *shaytan* made me forget to mention it – it miraculously made its way into the waters.'

He said, 'That is what we were looking for!'

So they went back the way they had come, and they found one of Our slaves to whom We had given mercy from Our presence, and to whom We had given knowledge straight from Us.

Musa said to him, 'May I follow you so that you can teach me about what you have been taught is right?'

He replied, 'Surely you will not be able to be patient with me – and how can you be patient with what you do not understand?'

He said, 'You will find that I am patient, *insh'Allah*, and I will not disobey you at all.

He replied, 'If you are going to follow me, then do not ask me about anything until I tell you about it.'

So the two set off, until, when they were being carried in a boat, he made a hole in it.

He (Musa) said, 'Have you made a hole in it so that its people will sink? – You have indeed done something terrible!'

He replied, 'Did I not tell you that you surely would not be able to be patient with me?'

He said, 'Do not be angry with me because I forgot, and do not be harsh with me because of my being difficult.'

So the two set off, until, when they met a young boy, he killed him.

He (Musa) said, 'Have you killed an innocent person who has not killed anyone? – You have indeed done something awful!'

He replied, 'Did I not say to you that you surely would not be able to be patient with me?'

He said, 'If I ask you about anything after this, then do not keep me in your company – you indeed have good reason because of me.'

So the two set off, until, when they came to the people of a town, they asked its people to feed them, but they refused to accept them as guests; and then they found a wall there which was about to fall down, and he repaired it.

He (Musa) said, 'If you had wanted, you could certainly have charged payment for this.'

He replied, 'This is the parting between me and you – I will now tell you the meaning of what you could not be patient with:

'As for the boat, it belonged to poor people who worked at sea, and I wanted to damage it because there was a king approaching them who had been seizing every boat by force.

'And as for the young boy, his parents were believers, and we feared that he would oppress them with wickedness and disbelief, and we wanted their Lord to exchange him for someone better than him who was pure and more likely to be merciful.

'And as for the wall, it belonged to two boys who were orphans in the town, and there was a treasure which was theirs under it, and their father had been a righteous man,

**and your Lord wanted them to reach their maturity and then reveal their treasure as a mercy from your Lord.**

**'And I did not do it of my own accord – that is the meaning of what you could not be patient with.'** (18.60-82).

Although Al-Khidr is not mentioned by name in the Qur'anic account, it is clear from the *hadith* transmitted by Ibn 'Abbas that it was indeed Al-Khidr whom *sayyedina* Musa met at the point where two seas meet, peace be on them, and that when *sayyedina* Musa asked Al-Khidr to teach him, he said, 'O Musa, I have some of the knowledge of Allah which Allah has taught me and which you do not know, and you have some of the knowledge of Allah which Allah has taught you and which I do not know.' When *sayyedina* Musa asked, 'May I follow you?' Al-Khidr replied, 'You will not be able to remain patient with me – how will you be able to remain patient about what you do not understand?' (Al-Bukhari).

According to the *hadith* transmitted by Ibn 'Abbas, while they were in the boat, a sparrow perched on the side of the boat and dipped its beak once or twice into the water. Al-Khidr said, 'O Musa, what I know and what you know has not decreased what Allah knows any more than the waters have been decreased by what the sparrow has drunk.' (Al-Bukhari).

According to the *hadith* transmitted by Ibn 'Abbas the Prophet Muhammad, may Allah bless him and grant him peace, concluded his account of what happened by saying, 'May Allah be merciful to Musa – if only he had remained patient, we would have heard more about their meeting!' (Al-Bukhari).

There has always been some debate as to whether Al-Khidr was a Prophet or a saint, especially since it is said that he has been given immortality and will never die. Allah knows best. Clearly, he was – or is – a man who possessed wisdom and who was rightly guided by Allah, and the lessons to be learned from the Qur'anic account are both many and profound.

There has also been some debate as to where 'the point where the two seas meet' is. Some say the two seas are the Red sea and the Mediterranean, others the Black sea and the Mediterranean, and still others that in this context the Arabic words *'majma'a al-bahrain'* refer to the point where two rivers, or even two lakes, meet. Thus some commentators, who think that the meeting between *sayyedina* Musa and Al-Khidr took place *before* the Tribe of Israel crossed the Red Sea, think that 'the point where the two seas meet' is where the White Nile and the Blue Nile meet. Allah knows best.

There is of course also the inner meaning of these words which is inherent in the account of what happened between *sayyedina* Musa and Al-Khidr, peace be on them, and which refers to the point where inward knowledge of Allah (*haqiqah*) meets the outward knowledge of what behaviour is necessary (*shari'ah*) – which is always to be found in and between those people who have been given knowledge by Allah.

It has been transmitted by Abu Hurayra, may Allah be pleased with him, that the Prophet Muhammad, may Allah bless him and grant him peace, said that Al-Khidr – which literally means 'the Green One' – was so named because after sitting on barren land, green plants grew where he had sat. (Al-Bukhari).

It has been transmitted by Abu Hurayra, may Allah be pleased with him, that the Prophet Muhammad, may Allah bless him and grant him peace, said that *sayyedina* Musa was a very modest man: his body was always covered and he always washed alone. One of the Tribe of Israel insinuated that this was because *sayyedina* Musa had leprosy or a hernia or some other defect, and Allah wished to clear him of this false allegation:

> One day, when *sayyedina* Musa, peace be on him, was going to have a bath in a secluded place, he put his clothes on a rock. After finishing washing himself, *sayyedina* Musa reached for his clothes – but the rock suddenly moved off, taking his clothes with it. *Sayyedina* Musa seized his staff and pursued the rock, shouting, 'Give me back my clothes, you stone!' but the rock did not stop until they reached a group of

people from the Tribe of Israel who then saw that *sayyedina* Musa had a most handsome body which had no defects of any kind. *Sayyedina* Musa picked up his clothes and put them on and then started hitting the rock with his staff. (Al-Bukhari).

The Prophet Muhammad, may Allah bless him and grant him peace, concluded his account of what happened by saying, 'By Allah, the stone still has traces of his beating it – three or four or five marks! And that is what the Most High is referring to when He says:

> **O you who believe, do not be like those who slandered Musa – when Allah cleared him of what they alleged – and he was well-regarded by Allah.' (33.69).**

It has been transmitted by Abu Hurayra, may Allah be pleased with him, that the Prophet Muhammad, may Allah bless him and grant him peace, said that *sayyedina* Musa was a tall man with brown skin and long straight hair. (Al-Bukhari).

It was during the period of forty years in which the Tribe of Israel were wandering in the wilderness that *sayyedina* Musa died, peace be on him. It is not certain exactly where he is buried, but it is said that he is buried near a red hill near Palestine, perhaps not far from the mountain where Allah first spoke to him, and where he received the revelation of the Taurah – Mount Tur – or Mount Sinai, as it is more commonly known as today.

Similarly, the Qur'an does not tell us when *sayyedina* Harun died, or where he is buried.

It has been transmitted by Abu Hurayra, may Allah be pleased with him, that the Prophet Muhammad, may Allah bless him and grant him peace, said that when the angel of death was sent to *sayyedina* Musa, peace be on him, *sayyedina* Musa hit the angel (whom *sayyedina* Musa did not recognise because he had appeared in the form of a human being) in the eye. The angel returned to his Lord and said, 'You have sent me to a slave who does not want to die.'

Allah replied, 'Go back to him and tell him to put his hand on the back of an ox, and for every hair that it covers, he will be given another year of life.' When the angel had done as he was told, *sayyedina* Musa asked what would happen after that, and he was told, 'Death,' so he said, 'Then let it come now,' and he asked Allah to let him die close to the Holy Land, only a stone's throw away.

According to Abu Hurayra, may Allah be pleased with him, the Prophet Muhammad, may Allah bless him and grant him peace, added, 'If I was there now, I could show you where his grave is, by the side of the road at the foot of a red sandhill.' (Al-Bukhari).

The importance and high station with Allah of *sayyedina* Musa and *sayyedina* Harun, peace be on them, should never be underestimated. Many thousands of years later, their influence can still be felt today. The standing of *sayyedina* Musa and *sayyedina* Harun with Allah is referred to in the following *ayat* from Surat as-Saffat:

> **And We were indeed generous towards Musa and Harun, and We delivered them and their people from the great distress, and helped them, so that they were the winners.**
>
> **And We gave them the Book which makes things clear, and We guided them on the straight path.**
>
> **And We left (the greeting) to them from those who came after: 'Peace be on Musa and Harun'.**
>
> **Surely that is how We reward those who do good – surely they were both from among Our trusting slaves. (37.114-122).**

It has been transmitted by Abu Hurayra, may Allah be pleased with him, that once a Muslim and a Jew started having an argument. The Muslim swore an oath, saying, 'By the One who preferred Muhammad, may Allah bless him and grant him peace, in all the worlds ...' and the Jew replied, 'By the One who preferred

Musa in all the worlds ...', whereupon the Muslim raised his hand and slapped the Jew, who then went to the Prophet Muhammad to complain:

The Prophet Muhammad, may Allah bless him and grant him peace, said, 'Do not say that I am better than Musa, because when everyone is struck senseless on the Last Day, I will be the first to regain my senses – only to see Musa holding on to the side of the Throne, and I will not know whether he was struck senseless and regained his senses before me, or whether he was one of those for whom Allah made an exception.' (Al-Bukhari).

There are many *ayat* in the Qur'an which refer to what happened to the Tribe of Israel after the death of *sayyedina* Musa. It is not possible to record all of them in this chapter, which is concerned primarily with the Prophet Musa himself, peace be on him, rather than with what happened to his followers after he had died, but the following *ayat* from Surat al-'Araf are instructive:

> **And among the people of Musa is a community who guide by the truth and establish justice by it.**
>
> **And We divided them into twelve tribes – communities – and when his people asked him for water, We inspired Musa to, 'Strike the rock with your staff!' and twelve springs gushed out from it, so that each tribe knew their drinking place; and We shaded them with clouds, and We sent down manna and quails for them, (saying), 'Eat of the good things with which We have provided you' – and they did not wrong Us, but they wronged themselves.**
>
> **And when it was said to them, 'Dwell in this town, and eat what you want from what is in it; and say, "Seeking forgiveness," and enter the gate prostrating; We will forgive you your wrong actions; We will give more to those who do good.'**
>
> **But those of them who did wrong changed the word to something other than what they had been told – so We sent**

**down a punishment on them from the sky because of their wrongdoing.**

(It has been transmitted by Abu Hurayra, may Allah be pleased with him, that the Prophet Muhammad, may Allah bless him and grant him peace, said that they 'changed the word' by entering the gate shuffling along on their bottoms instead of prostrating – and instead of saying, '*hittatun*' which means 'seeking forgiveness', they were saying, '*hibbatun fi sha'aratin*' which means 'a grain in the hair', or possibly, 'loving poetry'. (Al-Bukhari).)

**And ask them about the town which was beside the sea – how they broke the sabbath – how their fish openly came to them on the day they kept the sabbath, and on the day they did not keep the sabbath, they did not come to them. That is how We tested them, because they were disobedient.**

**And (remember) when a community of theirs said, 'Why are you warning a people whom Allah is about to destroy, or to punish with a mighty punishment?' they replied, 'To be free from blame before your Lord – and so that they may have *taqwa*.'**

**And when they forgot what they had been reminded of, We rescued those who forbade wrong and inflicted a dreadful punishment on those who did wrong because they were evil livers.**

**And when they took pride in (doing) what they had been forbidden, We said to them, 'Be apes, despised and loathed!'**

**And (remember) when your Lord proclaimed that He would certainly raise against them those who would inflict them with cruel torment until the Day of Standing – surely your Lord is swift in punishment, and surely He is Forgiving, Merciful.**

**And We have divided them up on the earth in (separate) communities; some of them are righteous – and some of them are far from that.**

**And We have tested them with good things and with evil things, so that perhaps they might return (to the straight path).**

**And a generation has succeeded them who have inherited the Book, who grasp at the goods of this low life and say, 'It will be forgiven us,' – and if a similar opportunity came to them, they would grasp at it (again).**

**Has not the covenant of the Book been made on their behalf that they should not say anything about Allah except the truth?**

**And they have studied what is in it. And the abode of the next life is better for those who have *taqwa*. Have you then no sense?**

**And as for those who hold fast to the Book, and establish the prayer – surely We do not let the reward of those who are righteous go to waste!**

**And (remember) when We made the mountain shake above them as if it were a shadow, and they thought that it would surely fall down on top of them, (and We said,) 'Take a firm hold of what We have given to you, and remember what is in it, so that you may have *taqwa*.'** (7.159-171).

Eventually the twelve tribes of the Tribe of Israel did settle in the Holy Land, in Palestine, and for thousands of years some, although not all, of them continued to live in accordance with the teachings of *sayyedina* Musa. There followed a long line of Prophets, peace be on all of them, who were sent by Allah to the Tribe of Israel to ensure that the teachings of *sayyedina* Musa were not altered, and – more significantly – to demonstrate how they were to be embodied.

As with all the Prophets and messengers before them, may the blessings and peace of Allah be on all of them, these Prophets – of whom only some are mentioned by name in the Qur'an – were accepted by some people and rejected by others.

It has been transmitted by Ibn 'Abbas, may Allah be pleased with him, that the Prophet Muhammad, may Allah bless him and grant him peace, once said, 'All the nations were shown to me, and I saw a huge multitude of people stretching to the horizon, and it was said, "This is Musa and his people."' (Al-Bukhari).

# CHAPTER TWO

## THE PROPHET HARUN
### peace be on him

As we have just seen in the preceding chapter, *sayyedina* Harun was the elder brother of *sayyedina* Musa, peace be on them. He was noted for his eloquence, which is why *sayyedina* Musa asked Allah for *sayyedina* Harun's company when he was commanded to go and invite Firaoun to only worship Allah. The life of *sayyedina* Harun was so closely linked to that of *sayyedina* Musa – although clearly there were periods when they were apart, during *sayyedina* Musa's childhood, for example, and during his time in Midian – that *sayyedina* Harun is never mentioned in the Qur'an without *sayyedina* Musa also being mentioned, except – as we shall see in Chapter Ten, on page 104, *insh'Allah* – where Maryam the mother of *sayyedina* 'Isa, peace be on them, is addressed as 'O sister of Harun', alluding to their common ancestry.

All the passages in the Qur'an which specifically refer to *sayyedina* Harun have already been quoted in the preceding chapter, with the exception of the following general *ayat* in which several Prophets are all mentioned together:

> **Surely We have inspired you (Muhammad) just as We inspired Nuh and the Prophets after him, as We inspired Ibrahim and Isma'il and Ishaq and Ya'qub and the tribes (of Israel) and 'Isa and Ayyub and Yunus and Harun and Sulayman, and Da'ud to whom We gave the *Zabur*, and Messengers whom we have told you about and Messengers whom we have not told you about, and Musa to whom Allah spoke directly – Messengers who brought good news and a warning so that mankind would not have any argument against Allah after the Messengers; and Allah has always been Mighty, Wise. (4.163-165).**

And, in Surat al-An'am, having described the argument which Ibrahim used against his people:

> **And We gave him (Ibrahim) Ishaq and Ya'qub, and We guided each of them – and before that We guided Nuh and, from among his descendants, Da'ud and Sulayman and Ayyub and Yusuf and Musa and Harun – and that is how We reward those who are good; and Zakariyya and Yahya and 'Isa and Ilyas – each of them was from among the righteous; and Isma'il and Alyassa' and Yunus and Lut – and We favoured each of them in all the worlds, as well as some of their forefathers and their descendants and their brothers; and We chose them and guided them to a straight path.**
>
> **Such is the guidance of Allah – by it He guides whomever of His slaves that He wants; but if they had worshipped other than Him, then all that they did would certainly have been in vain.**
>
> **These are the ones to whom We gave the Book and the wisdom and the prophethood; so if they disbelieve in it, then We will certainly entrust it to a people who do not disbelieve in it.**
>
> **These are the ones whom Allah guides – so follow their guidance. Say: 'I do not ask you for any reward for it. Surely it is only a reminder for all the worlds.'** (6.84-90).

There is also one other reference to *sayyedina* Harun in the Qur'an, peace be on him, in Surat al-Baqara, which is made in connection with the story of *sayyedina* Da'ud, peace be on him, and which is quoted in the next chapter, on page 61.

As has already been mentioned in the preceding chapter, one of the wives of the Prophet Muhammad, may the blessings and peace of Allah be on him and on his family and companions, Safiyya bint Huyayy, was descended from *sayyedina* Harun.

# Chapter Three

# The Prophet Da'ud
## peace be on him

*Sayyedina* Da'ud was descended from Judah, one of the twelve sons of *sayyedina* Ya'qub – who was otherwise known as Israel. *Sayyedina* Da'ud – who is known by the Jews and the Christians as the Prophet David – was one of the many Prophets who were sent to the Tribe of Israel after *sayyedina* Musa in order to keep his teachings alive, blessings and peace be on all of them:

> **Those of the Tribe of Israel who disbelieved were cursed by the tongue of Da'ud and of 'Isa son of Maryam – that is because they rebelled and exceeded the limits.**
>
> **They did not forbid each other the wrong they were doing – and what they used to do was certainly awful. (5.78-79).**

Indeed *sayyedina* Da'ud was a Messenger as well as a Prophet, since he was given a revelation to supplement the Taurah of *sayyedina* Musa, which was called the Zabur, and which is also known by the Jews and the Christians as the Psalms:

> **And your Lord knows best about whatever is in the heavens and the earth; and We certainly favoured some Prophets more than others; and We gave Da'ud the Zabur. (17.55).**

The references to *sayyedina* Da'ud in the Qur'an do not describe his childhood, but the *ayat* from Surat al-Baqara which follow do describe his killing the champion of the Philistines, Jalut, who is more commonly known by the Jews and the Christians as Goliath. The passage begins by describing the appointment of Talut – who fought and, with *sayyedina* Da'ud's help, overcame the Philistines – as the king of the Tribe of Israel by a Prophet of that time.

Although this Prophet is not named in the Qur'anic account, he has been identified with the Prophet who is known by the Jews and the Christians as the Prophet Samuel, while Talut has been identified with king Saul, the first king of the Tribe of Israel, who was descended from Ben Yamin (Benjamin) the son of Ya'qub, and who, it has been estimated, lived during the 11th century BC. Allah knows best:

**Have you considered (what happened) when the leaders of the Tribe of Israel after Musa asked a Prophet of theirs, 'Choose a king for us and we will fight in the way of Allah.'**

**He said, 'Is it possible that if you are commanded to fight, you will not fight?'**

**They replied, 'And why should we not fight in the way of Allah, when we and our children have been driven out from our homes?'**

**But when they were commanded to fight, they turned away – except for a few of them – and Allah is aware of those who do wrong.**

**And their Prophet said to them, 'Surely Allah has chosen Talut to be your king.'**

**They replied, 'Why should he have dominion over us when we have more right to the dominion than him, since he has not been given very much wealth?'**

**He said, 'Surely Allah has preferred him to you, and He has increased him abundantly in knowledge and in stature.'**

**And Allah gives dominion to whomever He wishes – and Allah is All-Encompassing, Knowing.**

**And their Prophet said to them, 'Surely the sign of his (right to) dominion will be that the Ark – in which there is tranquillity from your Lord, and the relics which the**

**family of Musa and the family of Harun left behind – will be brought to you, carried by the angels; surely in that there will certainly be a sign for you, if you are indeed believers.'**

(The Ark, which is said to have contained, *inter alia,* the tablets on which the Taurah was first inscribed, the staff of *sayyedina* Musa, and the staff of *sayyedina* Harun, had been captured by the Philistines years earlier. When the angels returned the Ark, the Tribe of Israel finally accepted Talut as their king, even though he was not descended from either Levi or Judah.)

**And when Talut set out with the army, he said, 'Surely Allah will test you at the river: for whoever drinks from it is not with me, and whoever does not taste it is surely with me – except for whoever only takes a handful in his hand.**

**And all but a few of them drank from it.**

**And when they had crossed over it, he and those who believed with him said, 'We will not be able to overpower Jalut and his forces today .'**

**But those who knew that they would surely be meeting Allah said, 'How often has a small army overcome a large army by the permission of Allah – and Allah is with those who are patient!'**

**And when they advanced against Jalut and his forces, they said, 'O our Lord, pour out patience on us, and make our foothold sure, and help us against the people who disbelieve.'**

**And they routed them by the permission of Allah, and Da'ud killed Jalut, and Allah gave him dominion and wisdom and taught him what He wished – and if Allah had not opposed some men by means of others, the earth would certainly have been corrupted, but Allah is Lord of generosity over all the worlds. (2.246-251).**

*Sayyedina* Da'ud, peace be on him, succeeded Talut as king of the Tribe of Israel, and during his rule all the tribes of the Tribe of Israel who had become divided were united again.

As well as being given the ability to link the twelve tribes of Israel together, *sayyedina* Da'ud was also given the knowledge of how to make chain-mail:

> **And We indeed gave Da'ud favours from Us, (saying), 'O you mountains and birds sing your praises with him!'**
>
> **And We made iron supple for him, so as to, 'Make long coats of mail and measure the links well – and do good – surely I am watching what you do.'** (34.10-11).

It has been transmitted by Abu Hurayra, may Allah be pleased with him, that the Prophet Muhammad, may Allah bless him and grant him peace, said that recitation was made easy for *sayyedina* Da'ud, peace be on him – so that he could give a command to his riding beast, let it loose and finish his recitation before his animal went off – and that he would only eat from what he had earned with the work of his own hands. (Al-Bukhari).

It has been transmitted by Ibn 'Umar, may Allah be pleased with him, that the Prophet Muhammad, may Allah bless him and grant him peace, said, 'The prayer which Allah loves most is that of Da'ud. The fast which Allah loves most is that of Da'ud. He used to sleep for half of the night, stand up in prayer for a third and sleep for a sixth. He would fast every other day. He wore wool and slept on hair. He ate barley bread with salt and ashes. He mixed his drink with tears. He was never seen to laugh after his error nor to look directly at the sky because of his shyness before his Lord and he continued to weep for the rest of his life. It is said that he wept until plants sprang up from his tears and until tears formed ridges in his cheeks. It is said that he went out in disguise to learn what people thought of him, and hearing himself praised only made him more humble.' (Al-Bukhari, Muslim, Ibn Hanbal, Abu Da'ud, An-Nasa'i, and Ibn Majah). (*Ash-Shifa'* of *Qadi* 'Iyad: 1.2.24).

The 'error' to which the above quotation from *Ash-Shifa'* of *Qadi* 'Iyad refers, concerns what is said to have happened between *sayyedina* Da'ud and the wife of Uriah – who is known by the Jews and the Christians as Bathsheba – and whom *sayyedina* Da'ud married after the death of Uriah, and who was the mother of *sayyedina* Sulayman – who is known to the Jews and the Christians as the Prophet Solomon – peace be on them. The following *ayat* from Surah Sad refer to whatever it was that happened:

**Be patient with what they say, and remember Our slave Da'ud, lord of might – surely he was always turning in repentance (to Allah).**

**Surely We subdued the mountains to glorify (Allah) with him at nightfall and at sunrise – and also the birds gathered together – all of them turned to Him in praise.**

**And We made his kingdom strong, and We gave him wisdom and sound judgement.**

**And have you heard the account of the litigants – how they climbed over the wall of the citadel and came in to Da'ud, frightening him, and they said, 'Do not be afraid – we are two litigants, one of whom has wronged the other, so judge between us with truth, and do not be unjust, and guide us to the right way:**

**'Surely this brother of mine had ninety-nine ewes, and I had one ewe, and he said, "Let me look after her," – and his proposal got the better of me.'**

**He (Da'ud) said, 'He has indeed wronged you by asking for your ewe in addition to his ewes, and surely many of those who bargain together certainly wrong each other, except for those who believe and do good – and how few they are!'**

**And Da'ud thought that We had surely been testing him, so he asked his Lord for forgiveness and fell down, bowing – and he repented.**

**And so We forgave him that – and surely he certainly has a near place in Our presence and a good destiny.**

**(And Allah said), 'O Da'ud, surely We have chosen you as a *khalif* in the earth, so judge between people with truth, and do not follow any desire that may lead you away from the way of Allah – surely those who go astray from the way of Allah will have an intense punishment, because they forgot about the Day of Reckoning.** (38.17-26).

In referring to this passage, *Qadi* 'Iyad states:

While the Prophet Da'ud was being ascetic and eating from the work of his own hands, he had ninety-nine wives and he completed the hundred by marrying Uriya's wife. Allah mentions that in His Mighty Book when He says, **'This brother of ours had ninety-nine ewes...'** (38.23). (*Ash-Shifa'* of *Qadi* 'Iyad: 1.2.8).

And:

As for the story of Da'ud, one only has recourse to what the traditionists have written about him which has been taken from the People of the Book who have altered and changed things. Allah does not give a text for any of it and it has not come down to us in any sound *hadith*.

What Allah says about the matter is contained in His words, **'Da'ud thought that We had only tested him; therefore he asked his Lord for forgiveness and fell down, bowing, and he repented. Accordingly We forgave him that, and he has a near place in Our presence and a fair resort.'** (38.24-25). In it, Allah says that he was 'repentant'. The meaning of Allah's testing him, is to try him. According to Qatada, repentant here means obedient, and this is the better interpretation.

Ibn 'Abbas and Ibn Mas'ud said that Da'ud only told the man to leave his wife with him so that he would be able to see that she was provided for. Allah censured him for that, warned him and objected to his preoccupation with this world. This cannot be relied on. It is said that he proposed to her when another man had already proposed to her. It is said that in his heart he wanted her husband to be killed.

As-Samarqandi said that his wrong action for which he asked forgiveness was his statement to one of the protagonists, **'He has wronged you,'** so that he considered him wronged merely by the statement of his adversary. It is said that he was fearful, thinking of the trial that had been opened up in front of him, of his kingdom and this world.

Ahmad ibn Nasr, Abu Tammam and other precise scholars believe that what these traditions ascribe to Da'ud should be refuted.

Ad-Da'udi has said that there is no confirmed report about the story of Da'ud and Uriah (Uriya') and that it is not permissible to suppose that a Prophet would want to kill another Muslim.

It is said that the two adversaries who argued before him really were arguing about a ewe, taking the *ayat* literally. **(***Ash-Shifa'* of *Qadi* 'Iyad: 3.1.13**)**.

And:

One of the *'ulama'* has said that the Prophets were punished for the slightest thing because of their position with Allah, while these things are ignored in the case of all other creatures since other people lack concern about them because of the extent of their bad behaviour. Those who argue that the Prophets are protected from all wrong actions say what we say, namely that the Prophets are taken to task for oversight and forgetfulness while others are not punished for it. They have a higher station, so their state in such matters is more reprehensible than the state of others.

However, you should know that the kind of punishment referred to here is not punishment as it is defined by others. We say that the Prophets are punished for their lapses in this world so that it will increase their degree. They are tested in this way so that their awareness of it will be a means for the raising of their degree as in the words of Allah, **'Then His Lord chose him and He turned to him and guided him.'** (20.122). **(***Ash-Shifa'* of *Qadi* 'Iyad: 3.1.14**)**.

And:

> One of the theologians said that the errors of the Prophets are outwardly errors, while in reality they are marks of honour and acts that bring nearness. This is like what we have already stated. Other people learn from the mistakes of the Prophets and those who do not have their degree take note of their punishment for what they did and are increased in awareness and caution and concern for taking account of their actions, so as to remain thankful for blessings and steadfast in afflictions by seeing what happened to the people of this high, protected level. This is why Salih al-Murri said that the case of Da'ud has been mentioned as a means of expansion for those who turn in repentance. (*Ash-Shifa'* of *Qadi* 'Iyad: 3.1:14).

As well as being one of the Prophets who is mentioned by name in the passages from Surat an-Nisa and Surat al-An'am which have already been quoted in Chapter Two, *sayyedina* Da'ud is also referred to in Surat al-Anbiyya, where Allah again refers to his and his son *sayyedina* Sulayman's ability to give judgement, peace be on both of them:

> **And (remember) when Da'ud and Sulayman both gave judgement concerning the field into which some people's sheep had strayed and grazed at night – and We witnessed the judgement they gave, and We gave Sulayman understanding of it – and We gave each of them wisdom and knowledge.**
>
> **And We subdued the mountains and the birds to glorify (Allah) with Da'ud – and it was We Who were doing it!**
>
> **And We taught him the art of making coats (of mail) for you, to protect you from being hurt – so will you be grateful? (21.78-80).**

It is said that in this case *sayyedina* Sulayman improved on the judgement of his father, even though he was only eleven years old at the time: Whereas *sayyedina* Da'ud initially decided that the sheep should be given to the owner of the field as compensation for the damage that they had caused, *sayyedina* Sulayman decided that the owner of the field should be allowed to keep the sheep until he had received full compensation from the flock – in the form of offspring, milk and wool – after which the sheep should be returned to their original owner.

It has also been transmitted by Abu Hurayra, may Allah be pleased with him, that the Prophet Muhammad, may Allah bless him and grant him peace, gave the following account of a case in which *sayyedina* Da'ud and then *sayyedina* Sulayman gave different judgements: 'There were two women, each of whom had a child with her. A wolf came along and took away the child of one of them, and so her companion said, "It has taken your child!" The other one said, "No, it has taken *your* child!" So they both presented their case to Da'ud, who judged in favour of the older woman. Then both of them went to Sulayman ibn Da'ud, peace be on them, and told him about it. He said, "Bring me a knife so that I can cut the child in half and share it between them!" The younger woman said, "Don't do it! may Allah have mercy on you – it is her child!" So he judged in favour of the younger woman.' (Al-Bukhari).

Another person to whom Allah gave wisdom during the lifetime of *sayyedina* Da'ud was Luqman. It is said that Allah gave him the choice between being a Prophet and being a wise man, and that he chose to be a wise man. It is said that he became the counsellor of *sayyedina* Da'ud, peace be on them. It is also said that Aesop's fables can be traced back to Luqman. Allah knows best. In the *surah* named after Luqman, Allah says:

> **And We indeed gave Luqman wisdom, (saying), 'Be grateful to Allah!' – and whoever is grateful is surely grateful for his own good, and as for whoever is ungrateful, then surely Allah is All-Sufficient, Worthy of Praise!'**
>
> **And (remember) when Luqman said to his son, as he was giving him advice, 'O my son, do not associate partners with Allah – surely associating partners (with Him) is certainly a great wrong.'**

**And We have commanded man concerning his parents – his mother carries him with weakness in weakness, and his weaning is within two years – to, 'Be grateful to Me and to your parents, and to Me is the journeying, and if they try to make you associate partners of whom you know nothing with Me, then do not obey them, and keep company with them in this world with kindness, and follow the path of those who turn to Me, and then you will return to Me, and I will tell you about what you were doing.'**

**'O my son, establish the prayer, and command what is good, and forbid what is evil, and be patient whatever happens to you – surely that is at the very heart of things – and do not make faces at people, and do not walk insolently in the land – surely Allah does not love anyone who is arrogant and conceited – and be moderate in your bearing, and lower your voice – surely the most hideous sound of all is the braying of an ass!'** (31.12-19).

It has been related that *sayyedina* Luqman said, 'My son, gold and silver are tested by fire and the believer is tested by affliction.' (*Ash-Shifa'* of *Qadi* 'Iyad: 3.2.9).

# Chapter Four

# The Prophet Sulayman
## peace be on him

As we have just seen in the preceding chapter, *sayyedina* Sulayman was the son of *sayyedina* Da'ud who was descended from Judah, one of the twelve sons of *sayyedina* Ya'qub – who was otherwise known as Israel. It is said that *sayyedina* Sulayman became the king of the Tribe of Israel when he was twelve years old. The wisdom of *sayyedina* Sulayman has become as proverbial as the patience of *sayyedina* Ayyub, peace be on them.

Like his father before him, *sayyedina* Sulayman was also tested by Allah:

> **And to Da'ud we granted Sulayman, an excellent slave – surely he was always turning in repentance (to Allah).**
>
> **(And remember) when he was presented with dancing, long-necked horses near nightfall ...**
>
> (It is said that *sayyedina* Sulayman was so captivated by their beauty that he forgot to do the prayer.)
>
> **And then he said, ' Surely I have found my love for the good things more pleasing than remembrance of my Lord, and now the sun has disappeared behind the horizon – bring them back to me!' – and then he began to slash at their legs and necks. (38.30-33).**

It has been transmitted by Abu Hurayra, may Allah be pleased with him, that the Prophet Muhammad, may Allah bless him and grant him peace, said, 'Sulayman the son of Da'ud said, "Tonight I will sleep with seventy wives, each of whom will bear a warrior who will fight in the way of Allah!" And his companion said to him, "*Insh'Allah*," but he did not say it, and no-one was made pregnant except for one wife who gave birth to half a child.' The Prophet, may Allah bless him and grant him peace, added, 'If he had said it, they would certainly have (all given birth to warriors who) fought in the way of Allah! (Al-Bukhari, who adds that Shu'aib and Ibn Abi az-Zinad, may Allah be pleased with them, said, 'Ninety (ladies) is more accurate.').

*Qadi* 'Iyad – who records that Ibn 'Abbas said that *sayyedina* Sulayman had three hundred wives (or, according to an-Naqqash and others, seven hundred wives) and three hundred slave-girls – states that the following *ayat* from Surah Sad may refer to the above incident:

> **And We indeed tested Sulayman – and We threw a (dead) body on his throne – and then he turned in repentance.**
>
> **He said, 'My Lord, forgive me and give me a kingdom the like of which no one else after me will ever have – surely You are the One Who gives!'**
>
> **And We made the wind subservient to him, pursuing its course as he wished, at his command, wherever he wanted; and also all the *shayatin* – as builders and divers – and others, bound in chains, (saying), 'This is Our gift – so give or withhold, without measure.'**
>
> **And surely he certainly has a near place in Our presence and a good destiny. (38.34-40).**

In referring to this passage, *Qadi* 'Iyad states:

> As for the story of Sulayman and what the commentators have related about his wrong action and Allah's statement, **'We tested (*fatanna*) Sulayman,' (38.34)** it means to put him to the test. He was afflicted, as the Prophet related, (in Muslim and Al-Bukhari and elsewhere), as follows: 'At night, he went around to a hundred wives (or ninety-nine) on a horse which he used for striving in the way of Allah. His friend said to him, "Say, 'If Allah wills.'" He did not say it and

only one of his wives became pregnant and she gave birth to half a child.' The Prophet said, 'By the One in Whose hand my soul is, if he had said, "If Allah wills," they would have striven in the way of Allah.'

The people of meanings say that 'half' means the dead body which was cast on his chair when it was shown to him and that was his punishment and test. It is said that the child died and was cast dead on his chair. It is said that his wrong action was avarice and desire. It is said that he did not say, 'If Allah wills,' when he was overwhelmed and overcome by desire.

It is said that his punishment was that his kingdom was stripped away and his wrong action was that he was tempted to judge unjustly in favour of one of his favourite wife's relations. It is said that he was punished for a wrong action into which one of his wives tempted him.

What the historians transmit about *shaytan* taking on the form of Sulayman, overcoming his kingdom, and governing his community with unjust rule is not true because the *shayatin* do not have this power and the Prophets were protected from things of this nature.

If the question is put: 'Why did Sulayman not say, "If Allah wills," in this story?' there are various answers. One is what is related in the sound *hadith* to the effect that he simply forgot to say it. That was so that the will of Allah would be carried out. The second is that he did not hear his companion and was distracted from him.

Sulayman said, **'Give me a kingdom that no one after me will have.' (38.35)**. Sulayman did not do this out of jealousy or desire for this world. His goal, according to the commentators, was that no one would have the power Sulayman was given in the same manner that *shaytan* seized that power when it was stripped from Sulayman in the period of his affliction. This is according to those who take that position.

It is said that he wanted it to be a sign of excellence and a special gift from Allah to him by which he would be singled out with special signs from Him.

It is said that it was in order that it be a proof and evidence of his prophethood in the same way that making iron soft was for his father, bringing the dead to life was for 'Isa, and like the special gift of intercession to Muhammad. (*Ash-Shifa'* of *Qadi* 'Iyad: 3.1.13).

And:

It is related that in spite of the great kingdom Sulayman was given, he did not lift his eyes towards heaven out of fear and humility towards Allah. He would feed people delicious foods while he ate barley bread. It was revealed to him: 'O leader of the worshippers and goal of the ascetics.' Once when he was riding on the wind among his armies, an old woman protested to him and he commanded the wind to stop so he could see what she needed before he went on. (*Ash-Shifa'* of *Qadi* 'Iyad: 1.2.24).

And:

In the *Sahih* Collections, Abu Hurayra said that the Prophet said, '*Shaytan* appeared to me in the form of a cat and attacked me in order to break my prayer, so Allah gave me power over him. I repelled him, grabbing him by the throat. I wanted to shackle him to a pillar so that you could look at him in the morning, but I remembered the words to my Lord of my brother Sulayman, **"Lord, forgive me and give me a kingdom that no-one after me should have. You are the Giving."'** (38.35). Allah drove him away a loser. (*Ash-Shifa'* of *Qadi* 'Iyad: 3.1.4). (The 'form of a cat' is an addition to what is in the *Sahih* and comes from 'Abdu'r-Razzaq ibn Hammam.)

It is clear from the Qur'an that the extent – both in area and in degree – of *sayyedina* Sulayman's kingdom, peace be on him, was extraordinary. As we have already seen, he was given power not only over people, but also over the wind, and therefore the weather, and over the *jinn*, as the following *ayat* also indicate:

**And We made the strong wind subservient to Sulayman, pursuing its course at his command to the land which We have blessed – and We are aware of everything.**

> **And also some of the *shayatin*, some of whom dived for him and some of whom did other kinds of work – and We were keeping watch over them. (21.81-82).**

And:

> **And We made the wind subservient to Sulayman – the morning breeze (lasted) a month and the evening breeze (lasted) a month – and We made a fountain of molten brass flow for him; and also some of the *jinn* to work at his command by the permission of his Lord – and We made whoever of them rebelled against Our command taste a burning punishment.**
>
> **They made whatever he wanted for him – places of worship, and works of art, and storage-places like wells, and cauldrons sunk into the ground, (and it was said), 'O family of Da'ud, work with gratitude!' – and few of My slaves are grateful. (34.12-13).**

It was thanks to the vast work force at his disposal, both in the Seen and the Unseen, that *sayyedina* Sulayman enjoyed such fabulous wealth and built such extraordinary edifices, of which perhaps the most famous was his temple, 'the Temple of Solomon' as it is still known today, which was built on the foundations of the place of worship in Jerusalem which is said to have been first built by *sayyedina* Ya'qub, some forty years after *sayyedina* Ibrahim had built the Ka'ba with the help of *sayyedina* Isma'il, may the blessings and peace of Allah be on them. It is also said that both of these places of worship were first built by *sayyedina* Adam, peace be on him, with a period of forty years between the two, and that *sayyedina* Ibrahim and *sayyedina* Ya'qub built on *sayyedina* Adam's foundations. Allah knows best.

As we shall see in a little more detail in the following chapters, *insh'Allah*, the Temple of *sayyedina* Sulayman was subsequently destroyed, rebuilt, and then destroyed again, so that today only its foundations – on or near which it is said the Masjid al-Aqsa now stands – remain.

It was either when the Temple was destroyed for the first time, or else certainly when it was destroyed for the second time, that the Ark – which, as we have already seen had been captured from the Tribe of Israel by the Philistines and then returned to king Talut by the angels, and which in the time of *sayyedina* Sulayman was kept in the inner sanctuary of the Temple – appears to have disappeared. Only Allah knows where it is today.

*Sayyedina* Sulayman's mastery over the creation was balanced by his knowledge and understanding of it. For example, the following excerpt from As-Suyuti's book on the medicine of the Prophet Muhammad, may Allah bless him and grant him peace, *Tibb an-Nabbi,* acknowledges *sayyedina* Sulayman's intimate knowledge of the plant world and its medical properties:

> A hadith that has been transmitted from al-Hassan through Qatada says that when Sulayman, peace be on him, had finished constructing the Temple, he entered the place of prayer, and suddenly there before him was a bush. When he had finished his prayers, the bush said, "Are you not going to ask me who I am?"
>
> And he replied, "Yes, who are you?" And the bush said, "I am a such-and-such bush, and a remedy for so-and-so, and this and that come from such and so." Then Sulayman ordered that the bush be cut down. And when this had been done, then suddenly another one, similar to it, grew up. And so every day, when he entered the place of prayer, he would meet another of these bushes. In this way he acquired a complete knowledge of all of them, and then wrote his book on Medicine about them, describing the remedies from them.
>
> There is a well-known hadith transmitted from Ibn Abbas that Sulayman, peace be on him, acquired his knowledge of plants as they grew in front of him. He would say to one, "What is your name?" And he would say to another, "What are you for?" And then, depending on their answers, if it was suitable to cultivate the species, cuttings from them would be replanted. And if one contained a remedy, then he would make a record of it. This hadith is taken from Abu Nu'aim. (*Tibb an-Nabbi* of As-Suyuti: 2.4).

Allah says in the Qur'an:

> **And there is not a creature that moves on the earth nor a creature that flies in the air with wings but that they are communities like you – We have not left out anything in the Book (of Creation) – and then they will be gathered to their Lord. (6.38).**

And:

> **Do you not see that whatever is in the heavens and the earth – including the birds in flight – glorifies Allah? He is certainly aware of the worship and praise of each of them – and Allah knows what they are doing. (24.41).**

*Sayyedina* Sulayman was not only fully aware of this, but also he, peace be on him, understood the languages of Allah's creatures, including not only the birds, but also the insects, as the following *ayat* from Surat an-Naml – which also describe how Bilqis, the Queen of Sheba, came to embrace Islam – make clear:

> **And We indeed gave knowledge to Da'ud and Sulayman – and they said, 'Praise to Allah, Who has been more generous to us than to many of His believing slaves!'**
>
> **And Sulayman was the heir of Da'ud, and he said, 'O people, we have been taught the language of the birds, and we have been given everything (in abundance) – surely this is certainly a distinct favour!'**
>
> **And (remember when) the armies of Sulayman from among the *jinn* and mankind and the birds were gathered around him and advancing in battle order until, when they reached the valley of the ants, an ant said, 'O ants, go into your dwellings, lest Sulayman and his armies crush you without realising it!'**
>
> **And he (Sulayman) smiled, laughing at its words, and said, 'My Lord, fill me with gratitude for the blessings with which You have favoured me and my parents, and make me**

**do good that is pleasing to You, and by Your mercy include me among Your righteous slaves.'**

**Andhe looked among the birds and said, 'How is it that I do not see the hoopoe, or is he not here? – I will certainly punish him with a severe punishment, or even execute him, unless he gives me a good excuse!'**

**But he was not long in coming, and said, 'I have just found out something which you do not know about – and I come to you from Saba with reliable news:**

(Saba, or Sheba, was a kingdom in southern Arabia, in southern Yemen, situated on the trade routes between Africa and India.)

**'Surely I have found out that there is a woman ruling over them, and she has been given everything (in abundance), and she has a mighty throne.**

**'I found her and her people prostrating in worship to the sun, instead of to Allah, and *shaytan* has made their actions seem attractive to them, and he has turned them away from the (right) way, and so they are not rightly guided – they do not prostrate before Allah, the One Who reveals what is hidden in the heavens and the earth, and Who knows what you conceal and what you make apparent – Allah – there is no god except Him, the Lord of the Mighty Throne.'**

**He (Solomon) replied, 'We shall see whether you have spoken the truth or if you are one of those who lie – go with this letter of mine and deliver it to them and then leave them and see what their response is.'**

**(When Bilqis received the letter), she said, 'O chieftains, surely I have received a noble letter; it is from Sulayman; and it begins, "In the Name of Allah the Merciful the Compassionate – do not exalt yourselves over me, but come to me as Muslims."'**

She said, 'O chieftains, counsel me in this matter – I will not decide anything until you have given me your advice.'

They replied, 'We are a powerful people and a people of great strength, but it is for you to command, so consider what your command will be.'

She said, 'Surely when kings enter a city, they ruin it and they humble its most powerful people – and that is what they will do – so I am going to send them a gift, to see what my messengers bring back.'

And when (her messenger) came to Sulayman, he said, 'Are you sending us wealth, when what Allah has given me is better than what He has given you? Indeed! – You are exalting yourselves through this gift of yours! Go back to them! – And we will most certainly come against them with forces which they cannot resist, and we will certainly drive them out from there, humbled and humiliated!'

Then he said, 'O chiefs, which of you can bring her throne here, before they come to me in submission?'

A demon from the jinn said, 'I will bring it to you before you can stand up from where you are sitting – surely I am certainly strong and trusty enough to do it!'

And one who had knowledge of the Book said, 'I will bring it to you before your glance can return to you!'

And when he (suddenly) saw it standing in front of him, he (Sulayman) said, 'This is by the generosity of my Lord, so that he can test me as to whether I am grateful or ungrateful – and whoever is grateful is surely grateful for his own good, and as for whoever is ungrateful, then surely my Lord is All-Sufficient, Generous.'

He said, 'Disguise her throne for her so that we can establish whether she will be rightly guided, or whether she is one of those who are not rightly guided.'

**And when she arrived, it was said to her, 'Is your throne like this one?'**

**She replied, 'It is just like it!'**

**And (it was said), 'We were given knowledge before her, and we were Muslims. And what she used to worship instead of Allah led her astray – surely she was from a people who disbelieved.'**

**It was said to her, 'Come into the palace,' – and when she saw it, she thought it was a pool of water, and she bared her legs.**

**He (Sulayman) said, 'It is only a palace paved with glass!'**

**She said, 'My Lord, surely I have wronged myself – and I submit, with Sulayman, to Allah, Lord of the worlds.' (27.15-44).**

After her acceptance of Islam, *Sayyedina* Sulayman subsequently married Bilqis, thereby extending his kingdom still further.

It is not surprising – since *sayyedina* Sulayman's dominion was not only exercised in the worlds which are apprehended by the senses but also extended into the Unseen worlds as well – that there has been some speculation about this by those whose knowledge and perception of what is in the Unseen are limited.

This is true even concerning what has been said about what is stated in the Qur'an, especially the *ayat* which follow, and accordingly it would be helpful to also consider what a reliable *faqih* such as *Qadi* 'Iyad has said about the matter. The *ayat* in question are to be found in Surat al-Baqara:

**And they follow what the *shayatin* taught during the reign of Sulayman.**

**And Sulayman did not disbelieve, but it was the *shayatin* who disbelieved, teaching people magic and what was re-**

**vealed to the two angels in Babel – Harut and Marut – and they did not teach it to anyone until they had said, 'Surely we are only a test, so do not disbelieve.'**

**And from these two they have learned how to cause separation between a man and his wife – and they can not harm anyone with it except by the permission of Allah – and they have only learned what is harmful for them, and not what is beneficial for them; and they certainly know that whoever deals in it will not have any share of good in the next life, and certainly what they have sold their selves for is awful – if only they knew.**

**And if only they had believed and had *taqwa*, their reward from Allah would certainly have been better – if only they knew. (2.102-103).**

In referring to this passage – while considering the degree to which angels are protected from wrong action – *Qadi* 'Iyad states:

Something that those who do not consider it necessary for all angels to be protected use as a proof, is what is said in the traditions and commentaries regarding the story of Harut and Marut and what 'Ali and Ibn 'Abbas related about them and their temptation. You should know that these reports do not relate anything, either weak or sound, from the Messenger of Allah himself and there is nothing which is taken by analogy. The commentators disagree about the meaning of what the Qur'an says about them.

What one of them stated was rejected by many of the *Salaf* as we will show. These reports are taken from the books of the Jews and from their fabrications. What Allah told us about at the beginning of the passage concerned their forging lies like that against Sulayman and their declaring him to be an unbeliever. That story contains an immense atrocity. We will deal with that by removing the cover from these ambiguities, Allah willing.

Scholars disagree about whether Harut and Marut were angels or men and whether they are meant as 'two angels'. Is the recitation truly 'two angels (*malakayn*)' (as is found in the

Seven Readings of the Qur'an) or is it 'two kings (*malikayn*)' (as found in a rare reading from al-Hasan al-Basri)?

Are Allah's words **'What was sent down'** or are they **'It was not sent down** (*ma unzila*)'? Is **'They do not teach anyone'** (which could also be taken to be **'What they teach to anyone** (*ma yu'alimani*)**'**) negative or affirmative?

Most of the commentators believe that Allah tested people by the two angels who instructed them in magic, making it clear that the use of magic amounts to disbelief. Whoever learns it disbelieves and whoever leaves it believes.

Allah quotes them as saying, **'We are a trial, so do not disbelieve.' (2.102)** They taught magic to people with a warning, i.e. they told those who came to learn it, 'Do not do it. It parts a man and his wife. Do not suppose that it is good. It is magic, so do not disbelieve.'

According to this interpretation, what the two angels did was an act of obedience and they acted as Allah had commanded them. It was not rebellion. It was a trial for others.

Ibn Wahb has related that Khalid ibn Abi 'Imran mentioned Harut and Marut as teaching magic. Ibn Wahb added, 'We absolve them of this.' One of the scholars recited the verse as meaning, **'It was not sent down on the two angels.' (2.102)**. Khalid took this position and he possessed both esteem and knowledge. He absolved them even from teaching the magic which other scholars said that they had permission to teach provided that they made it clear that it was disbelief and a test and trial from Allah. How is it possible to do anything other than absolve them from all major wrong actions, acts of rebellion and the disbelief mentioned in these traditions? Khalid, as well as Ibn 'Abbas, said that the verse is a negative statement.

Makki said that the implication of the words, **'Sulayman did not disbelieve,'** means that he did not disbelieve by believing the magic which the *shayatin* fabricated against him and which the Jews followed, and he said that the two angels were Jibril and Mika'il.

The Jews allege that the two angels did that, just as they also claim that Sulayman used magic. Allah calls them liars: **'But the *shayatin* disbelieved and taught people magic, and that which was sent down on the two angels/kings at Babel,**

> **Harut and Marut.'** (2.102). It is said that they were two men who disbelieved. As-Sakan said that Harut and Marut were two infidels from the people of Babel. He must have recited 'What was sent down on the two kings' by this interpretation. 'Abdu'r-Rahman ibn Abza said that the two kings were Da'ud and Sulayman. As-Samarqandi said that they were two kings from the Banu Isra'il whom Allah transformed. The recitation as *'malikayn* (two kings)', however, is rare.
>
> The interpretation of the *ayat* according to the evaluation of Abu Muhammad Makki is good. It absolves the angels and removes impurity from them and considers them absolutely pure. Allah described them as being purified and **'Noble, good.'** (80.16). **'They do not rebel against Allah in what He commands them.'** (66.6). (*Ash-Shifa'* of *Qadi* 'Iyad: 3.1.16).

As well as being one of the Prophets who is mentioned by name in the passages from Surat an-Nisa and Surat al-An'am which have already been quoted in Chapter Two, *sayyedina* Sulayman is also referred to again in Surah Saba, when it describes the manner of his death. It is said that *sayyedina* Sulayman, peace be on him, died while he was leaning on his staff, and that the *jinn* who had been working under his supervision did not realise that he was dead until a termite had nibbled away the end of his staff which had continued to support his dead body, thereby causing it to topple over:

> **And when We decreed death for him, his death was only made apparent by an insect from the earth which nibbled away at his staff – and when (his body) toppled over, the *jinn* clearly realised that if only they had known the Unseen, they would not have continued doing the punishing work they hated! (34.14).**

It was not until much later that the people of Saba went astray and accordingly tasted what happens to those who do go astray:

> **There was indeed a sign for those who lived in Saba – two gardens, on the right and the left – (who were told), 'Eat from what your Lord has provided, and be grateful to him,' – a fortunate land and a forgiving Lord.**

**But then they turned away, so We set loose the flood from the dam of 'Iram on them, and We changed their two gardens into two gardens producing bitter fruit, with a few tamarisks and lote-trees.**

**That is how We paid them for their disbelief – and how else could We repay disbelief?**

**And We had placed towns which were easy to see between them and the cities which We have blessed, and We had measured the distance between them well for travelling, (saying), 'Travel between them in safety, by night or by day.'**

**But they said, 'Our Lord, increase the length of our journeys,' and they wronged themselves, and so We made them history, and We completely scattered all of them – surely in that there are certainly signs for everyone who is patient and grateful.**

**And what *shaytan* thought about them was indeed confirmed, for they followed him, except for a group of believers; and he had not been given any authority over them, except so that We could distinguish between whoever believes in the next world and whoever is in doubt about it – and your Lord keeps watch over everything. (34.15-21).**

It is interesting to note in passing that traces of the remains of the dam of 'Iram which engulfed the ancient city of Ma'rib – which is said to be the city from which Bilqis originally came – still exist to this day. The French traveller, T J Arnaud, for example, visited both the remains of the dam wall up in the mountains and the ruined city below, in 1843, and concluded that the dam must have been colossal. It has been estimated that the dam of 'Iram was destroyed in about 120 CE.

It has been estimated that *sayyedina* Da'ud ruled from approximately 1,000 to 960 BC, and that his son *sayyedina* Sulayman ruled from approximately 960 to 922 BC. Under their combined rule, therefore, peace be on them, the twelve tribes of the Tribe of Israel were united in one kingdom under rightly-guided prophetic rule for almost a century.

After the death of *sayyedina* Sulayman, however, this unity was destroyed, and the kingdom split between north and south, with some of the Tribe of Israel holding fast to the teachings of *sayyedina* Musa and *sayyedina* Da'ud, peace be on them, and others abandoning them and turning to idol-worship of one form or another instead.

A succession of Prophets followed, one after another – accepted by some, rejected by others, and at times even killed for calling the people of the Tribe of Israel to follow the Taurah and the Zabur and to only worship Allah.

Two of the Prophets who were sent principally to the people of the northern kingdom, during the 9th century BC, and who are mentioned in the Qur'an, were *sayyedina* Ilyas (who is said to be the Prophet who is known by the Jews and the Christians as the Prophet Elias, or Elijah) and his immediate follower *sayyedina* Alyassa' (who is said to be the Prophet who is known by the Jews and the Christians as the Prophet Elisha).

It should be emphasised that this pattern of acceptance and rejection of the Prophets sent by Allah to the Tribe of Israel was to be found in both the northern and the southern kingdoms, although it is interesting to note in passing that since all the major Prophets who were descended from the sons of *sayyedina* Ya'qub were descended either from his son Levi, or from his son Judah, it is probably for this reason that the leaders of these two tribes, along with some of the leaders of the tribe of *sayyedina* Ben Yamin (Benjamin) – from whom, it will be remembered, king Talut had been descended – eventually decided that they were the rightful inheritors and guardians of the teachings of *sayyedina* Musa – to the exclusion of the other nine and a half tribes of the Tribe of Israel, who were largely settled in the northern kingdom, and who were subsequently written out of 'Jewish' history by the historians of the southern kingdom.

Almost the last we hear of the nine and a half tribes in the north is in the context of the Assyrian invasion of the northern kingdom which took place in approximately 722 BC, and which resulted, it is claimed by Jewish historians, in the almost total annihilation of the tribes in the northern kingdom, with the exception of some 27,000 captives who were taken back as slaves to Nineveh, the ancient Assyrian capital at that time, situated on the banks of the river Tigris, opposite the site of today's city of Mosul in northern Iraq, and almost due north of Babylon, which was situated on the banks of the river Euphrates, a little way due south of today's city of Baghdad in central Iraq.

Even if the members of the nine and a half tribes were completely annihilated by the Assyrians in the 8th century BC – a claim which the results of serious and impartial research make it difficult to accept – it is clear that Allah did continue to send Prophets to the members of the Tribe of Israel who had been taken in captivity to Nineveh. Perhaps the most well-known of these Prophets was *sayyedina* Yunus (who is said to be the Prophet who is known by the Jews and the Christians as the Prophet Jonah), peace be on him and them.

# CHAPTER FIVE

# THE PROPHET ILYAS
## peace be on him

*Sayyedina* Ilyas was descended from *sayyedina* Harun, the brother of *sayyedina* Musa, who, as we have already seen, was descended from Levi, one of the twelve sons of *sayyedina* Ya'qub – who was otherwise known as Israel. *Sayyedina* Ilyas was one of the many Prophets who were sent to the Tribe of Israel after *sayyedina* Musa in order to keep his teachings alive, may the blessings and peace of Allah be on all of them.

It is said that *sayyedina* Ilyas was the Prophet who is also known by the Jews and the Christians as the Prophet Elias, or Elijah. Allah knows best.

As well as being one of the Prophets who is mentioned by name in the passage from Surat al-An'am which has already been quoted in Chapter Two, *sayyedina* Ilyas, peace be on him, is also referred to in Surat as-Saffat:

> **And surely Ilyas was certainly one of the Messengers, when he said to his people, 'Will you not have *taqwa*? Why do you pray to Ba'al and turn away from the Best of creators, Allah – your Lord and the Lord of your forefathers?'**
>
> **But they denied him, and so surely they will certainly be gathered together (to be punished) – except for the sincere slaves of Allah.**
>
> **And We left (the greeting) to him from those who came after: 'Peace be on Ilyas'.**
>
> **Surely that is how We reward those who do good – surely he was one of Our believing slaves.** (37.123-132).

# CHAPTER SIX

## THE PROPHET ALYASSA'
### peace be on him

*Sayyedina* Alyassa' was descended from *sayyedina* Ilyas, who, as we have just seen, was descended from *sayyedina* Harun, the brother of *sayyedina* Musa, who was descended from Levi, one of the twelve sons of *sayyedina* Ya'qub – who was otherwise known as Israel.

*Sayyedina* Alyassa' was one of the many Prophets who were sent to the Tribe of Israel after *sayyedina* Musa in order to keep his teachings alive, may the blessings and peace of Allah be on all of them.

It is said that *sayyedina* Alyassa' was the Prophet who is also known by the Jews and the Christians as the Prophet Elisha. Allah knows best.

As well as being one of the Prophets who is mentioned by name in the passage from Surat al-An'am which has already been quoted in Chapter Two, *sayyedina* Alyassa', peace be on him, is also referred to in Surah Sad:

> **And remember Isma'il and Alyassa' and Dhu'l Kifli – and each of them was from among those who are chosen. (38.48).**

# Chapter Seven

# The Prophet Yunus
## peace be on him

*Sayyedina* Yunus was descended from *sayyedina* Sulayman, the son of *sayyedina* Da'ud who was descended from Judah, one of the twelve sons of *sayyedina* Ya'qub – who was otherwise known as Israel – may the blessings and peace of Allah be on all of them.

*Sayyedina* Yunus was one of the many Prophets who were sent to the Tribe of Israel after *sayyedina* Musa in order to keep his teachings alive.

It is said that *sayyedina* Yunus, who is also called Dhu'n-Nun in the Qur'an, meaning 'he of the fish' – and referring to his having been swallowed by a large fish – was the Prophet who is also known by the Jews and the Christians as the Prophet Jonah, who was sent by king Hizkia to call the members of the Tribe of Israel who were in exile in Nineveh back to Allah. Allah knows best.

It is said that when *sayyedina* Yunus, peace be on him, first called on his people to turn to Allah, they ignored him, and that he told them that they would be punished by Allah after forty days. It is said that towards the end of this period, they turned to Allah in repentance, and accordingly they were not punished. It is said that *sayyedina* Yunus then left in anger, and that he caught a ship which was either overloaded, or would not move, or was caught in a violent storm, or all three, and that after casting lots with the other passengers, he lost the draw and had to jump overboard, whereupon he was swallowed by a large fish:

> **And surely Yunus was certainly one of the Messengers – (and remember) when he ran away to the overloaded ship, and cast lots, and he was the one who was held to blame, and so the fish swallowed him while he was at fault.**

**And if he had not been one of those who glorify (Allah), he would certainly have remained in its belly until the Day of Rising.**

**And then We threw him up on the empty shore, and he was ill, so we made a tree of gourds grow over him.**

**And We sent him to a hundred thousand people or more, and they believed, and so We gave them a good life for a while. (37.139-148).**

The following *ayat* also refer to *sayyedina* Yunus, peace be on him, describing how he turned to his Lord in repentance as he lay in the darkness of the fish's belly, in the darkness of the sea, in the darkness of the night:

**And (remember) when Dhu'n-Nun went off in anger, thinking that We would have no power over him – but then he called out in the darkness, saying, 'There is no god except You – glory be to You – surely I have been a wrong doer!'**

**And We listened to him, and We saved him from his affliction – and that is how We save those who believe. (21.87-88).**

And:

**So wait patiently for the decree of your Lord, and do not be like he of the fish, when he called out in despair.**

**If the blessing of his Lord had not reached him, he would certainly have been thrown up onto the empty shore in disgrace.**

**But his Lord chose him and put him among the righteous. (68.48-50).**

As well as being one of the Prophets who is mentioned by name in the passages from Surat an-Nisa and Surat al-An'am which have already been quoted in Chapter Two, *sayyedina* Yunus is also referred to again in the *surah* which is named after him, Surah Yunus:

> **And if only there had been a community (in the past) that believed, and benefited from its belief, like the people of Yunus – for when they believed, We removed the punishment of being disgraced in the life of this world from them, and We gave them a good life for a while.**
>
> **And if your Lord had wanted, all of those who are in the earth would have believed together.**
>
> **So, can you force people to be believers?**
>
> **And it is not for any self to believe except by the permission of Allah – and He has made those who have no intellect squalid.**
>
> **Say: 'Consider what is in the heavens and the earth!'**
>
> **But signs and warnings are of no use to people who will not believe. (10.98-101).**

In referring to the passages which have been quoted above, *Qadi* 'Iyad states:

> Another thing brought up by people desiring to make trouble is the story of Yunus when he threatened his people with punishment from their Lord. When they turned in repentance, the punishment was removed from them. He said, 'I will never return to them as a liar,' and left in anger.
>
> Know that none of the reports related about this subject say that Yunus actually said to them, 'Allah will destroy you.' What is said is that he called for their destruction. A supplication is not the same as a report which must be truthful. He said to them, 'May the punishment come to you in the morning at such-and-such a time.' Then Allah removed the punishment from them and prevented it from reaching them. Allah says about it, **'The people of Yunus believed, so We removed the punishment of humiliation from them.'** (10.98).

It is related in tradition by Ibn Mas'ud that Yunus saw signs and visions of the punishment. Sa'id ibn Jubayr said that the punishment was covering them as a cloth covers the grave. (*Ash-Shifa'* of *Qadi* 'Iyad: 3.1.6).

And:

As for his statement, **'I was one of the unjust,'** (21.87) injustice (*dhulm*) means to put something in other than its proper place. According to some of them, that is his admission of his wrongaction. As for his leaving his people without the permission of his Lord or because of his weakness regarding what he was made to bear or his calling for punishment against his people, Nuh called for the destruction of his people and was not punished.

Al-Wasiti said, 'He was disconnecting his Lord from injustice and ascribing the action to himself, acknowledging it as his just deserts. His statement is like that of Adam and Hawwa', **'Our Lord, we have wronged ourselves,'** (7.23) since they were the cause of their being in a place other than where they had first been put. They themselves were responsible for their expulsion from the Garden and their descent to the earth.' (*Ash-Shifa'* of *Qadi* 'Iyad: 3.1.13).

And:

Allah says about Yunus, **'He thought that We would have no power over him,'** (21.87) meaning : 'We would not constrict him.' Makki said that he desired the mercy of Allah and hoped that He would not make it difficult for him when he left. It was said that he had the good opinion of his Lord that He would not exact punishment from him. It is said that it means : 'We will give others power over him.' It is said that it means : 'We will punish him for his anger and departure.'

'Abdu'r-Rahman ibn Zayd said that it means : 'Did he think that We would not have power over him?' It is not fitting to think that a Prophet would be ignorant of one of his Lord's attributes. It is the same when He says, **'When he went out in anger.'** (21.87).

> The sound position is that he was angry with his people because of their disbelief as Ibn 'Abbas, ad-Dahhak and others said. His anger was not directed at his Lord since anger at Allah amounts to opposition to Him. Opposition to Allah is disbelief. It is not proper for the believers, so how could it be proper for the Prophets? (*Ash-Shifa'* of *Qadi* 'Iyad: 3.1.1).

It has been transmitted by Abu Hurayra, may Allah be pleased with him, that the Prophet Muhammad, may Allah bless him and grant him peace, said, 'No one should try to say that I am better than Yunus ibn Matta.' (Al-Bukhari).

There is no further direct reference in the Qur'an to what happened to the people of Yunus after his death, peace be on him. It is reasonable to conclude, however, that many of them continued to follow the Taurah and the Zabur until the coming of *sayyedina* 'Isa, peace be on him, and that many of them subsequently followed him, until the coming of *sayyedina* Muhammad, may Allah bless him and grant him peace, and that many of them subsequently embraced Islam and followed him.

This would then explain why the historians of the two and a half tribes of the Tribe of Israel in the southern kingdom – who became known as the Judahites – subsequently claimed that the members of the other nine and a half tribes of the Tribe of Israel in the northern kingdom – who became known as the Israelites – were either totally annihilated by the Assyrians in about 722 BC, or else 'disappeared' from history during their exile in Nineveh.

The only logical explanation for the history of the nine and a half tribes of the Tribe of Israel in the northern kingdom – which was called Israel – being excluded from what became known as 'the history of the Jews' is that it was because so many of them recognised and followed the last two major Prophets, *sayyedina* 'Isa and *sayyedina* Muhammad, may the blessings and peace of Allah be on them, whereas so many of the members of the two and a half tribes of the Tribe of Israel in the southern kingdom – which was called Judah – rejected them.

One of the most significant events in what became known as 'the history of the Jews' – that is, the history of only two and a half of the twelve tribes of the Tribe of Israel, who first came to be called 'the Judahites' and then 'the Jews' – occurred in approximately 586 BC, when king Nebuchadnezzar of Babylon and his forces completely overwhelmed the southern kingdom of Judah, utterly destroying the Temple of Solomon, and taking many of its inhabitants back to Babylon as captives.

It is significant that the consequences of this conquest appear to have been completely unlike those which have been attributed to the Assyrian conquest of the northern kingdom.

It is accepted by the vast majority of historians that certainly after – if not before – the sacking of Jerusalem by Nebuchadnezzar in 586 BC and the enforced exile of some of its inhabitants to Babylon, the original Taurah ceased to exist in its entirety. It is also accepted that the copies of the version which Ezra is alleged to have subsequently compiled from memory in Babylon were destroyed during the invasion of Jerusalem by Antiochus in 161 BC.

Thus, for example, Maulana M. Rahmatullahi Kairanvi, in his book *Izhar-ul-Haq*, quotes the nineteenth century Catholic scholar, John Mill, as stating:

> All the scholars unanimously agree that the original Torah (Pentateuch) and other original books of the Old Testament were destroyed by the forces of Nebuchadnezzar. When the books were recompiled through Ezra, these too were later on destroyed during the invasion of Antiochus.

Thus by the time the Taurah was first translated into Greek by seventy-two scholars in Alexandria between approximately 275 BC and 150 BC, the Hebrew version had already been re-written 'from memory' twice.

(The Talmud, which is alleged to record the oral traditions of Moses, did not actually appear in written form until some seventeen centuries after the death of Moses, and at least nine centuries after the Torah itself had ceased to exist in its original form:

The Mishnah, the written form of the alleged oral traditions of Moses was not collated in its present form until the beginning of the third century CE. The two commentaries on the Mishnah, the Jerusalem Gemara and the Babylonian Gemara, were not completed until the fifth and seventh centuries CE respectively, while the commentaries written on these commentaries, the very extensive Midrash literature, were written between 400 and 1200 CE.)

The exile in Babylon lasted for about fifty years. King Cyrus of Persia conquered Babylon in 538 BC, and permitted the exiles to return to Jerusalem. Some of them returned almost immediately, and set about rebuilding the Temple of Solomon, which was completed in about 515 BC, while others went back in about 458 BC, led by Ezra, who was later joined by Nehemiah, the Persians' appointee as governor of Judah.

It is said that one of the reasons for Ezra's delay in returning to Jerusalem was that he was busy writing down the Taurah from memory, although it is clear from even a brief look at the five books of the Pentateuch – which is usually alleged to be the same as the Taurah which was revealed to *sayyedina* Musa – that they contain historical accounts of what is alleged to have happened both during and after the life of *sayyedina* Musa, peace be on him, and which therefore cannot possibly be part of the original revelation of the Taurah which *sayyedina* Musa received from Allah.

During the next four centuries, from 450 to 50 BC, and especially after the destruction of Ezra's compilations by Antiochus in his invasion of Jerusalem in 161 BC, the book which was called the Taurah – together with the additional books which purported to record the history of the Tribe of Israel after the time of *sayyedina* Musa, and which were often written and compiled from fragments centuries after the events which they purported to describe had taken place – continued to be revised and rewritten, and what was to become the religion of Judaism began to take definite shape, headed by a strong Levitical priesthood who regarded themselves as the rightful guardians of this ancient knowledge.

During the same period, from 450 to 50 BC, there was a succession of different occupying forces in the Holy Land, including Alexander the Great and the Greeks and culminating with the Romans, who by 63 BC had effective control of Jerusalem.

In other words, ever since the invasions of the Assyrians in 722 BC, and of Nebuchadnezzar in 586 BC, there had been a series of struggles for both political and religious control and power in both the north and the south of the Holy Land, none of which could be particularly described as being in harmony with the original teachings of *sayyedina* Musa, peace be on him.

As time passed, and as circumstances became more extreme, there was a growing expectation amongst those who still believed and trusted in Allah that the prophecies about the coming of a new Messiah, a new Messenger from Allah, which had been contained in the original Taurah – even if they were no longer to be found in their original form in the rewritten version – were soon to be fulfilled.

It was into this situation that the two Prophets who were to directly precede *sayyedina* 'Isa were born, *sayyedina* Zakariyya and *sayyedina* Yahya.

# Chapter Eight

# The Prophet Zakariyya
## peace be on him

*Sayyedina* Zakariyya was descended from *sayyedina* Sulayman, the son of *sayyedina* Da'ud who was descended from Judah, one of the twelve sons of *sayyedina* Ya'qub – who was otherwise known as Israel, peace be on them. It is clear that *sayyedina* Zakariyya was the man who is known by the Jews and the Christians as Zachariah.

The significance of *sayyedina* Zakariyya lies in the fact that he was the guardian of Maryam, the mother of *sayyedina* 'Isa, and he was also the father of *sayyedina* Yahya who was the first to openly proclaim the coming of *sayyedina* 'Isa, peace be on them.

The mother of Maryam was called Hannah and her father, who was descended from *sayyedina* Sulayman, was – like the father of *sayyedina* Musa – called 'Imran, peace be on them. Before Maryam was born, Hannah vowed that she would give the child she was carrying as an offering for the service of Allah. Thus when Maryam was still a small child, she was taken by Hannah to the Temple in Jerusalem, where it was decided – after lots had been cast – that *sayyedina* Zakariyya should be her guardian:

> **Surely Allah chose Adam and Nuh and the family of Ibrahim and the family of 'Imran above all the worlds – they were descended from each other – and Allah is Hearing, Knowing.**
>
> **(And remember) when the wife of 'Imran said, 'My Lord, surely I have vowed that what is in my womb will be dedicated to You – so accept it from me. Surely it is You Who are the Hearer, the Knower.'**

And when she had given birth to her, she said, 'My Lord, surely I have given birth to a girl,' and Allah knew best to whom she had given birth – a boy is not like a girl – 'and surely I have named her Maryam, and surely I seek protection in You for her and her offspring from the outcast *shaytan.*'

And her Lord accepted her with complete acceptance, and made her grow in complete health, and made Zakariyya her guardian.

And whenever Zakariyya entered the sanctuary where she was, he found that she had food. He said, 'O Maryam, from where has this come?'

She replied, 'It is from Allah – surely Allah provides for whomever He wishes without reckoning.'

Then Zakariyya prayed to his Lord, saying, 'My Lord, grant me good offspring from Your presence – surely You hear prayer.'

And the angels called to him as he stood in prayer in the sanctuary, 'Surely Allah gives you good news of Yahya, who will confirm a Word ('Isa) from Allah, and who will be honourable and chaste and one of the righteous Prophets.'

He said, 'My Lord, how can I have a son, when I have become old and my wife is barren?'

He replied, 'Just like that – Allah does what He wants.'

He said, 'My Lord, give me a sign.'

He replied, 'Your sign shall be that you will not speak to anyone for three days except by sign-language – and remember your Lord much and glorify Him at nightfall and in the early morning.'

**And (remember) when the angels said, 'O Maryam, surely Allah has chosen you, and He has made you pure, and He has preferred you above all women in all the worlds. O Maryam, be obedient to your Lord, and prostrate and bow down in worship (before Him) with those who bow down in worship.' This is from tidings of the Unseen which We reveal to you – and you were not there with them when they cast their reeds (to decide) which of them should be Maryam's guardian, and you were not there with them when they argued about it. (3.33-44).**

It is said that it was because of Hannah's prayer for Maryam and her offspring that *shaytan* could not touch either her or *sayyedina* 'Isa when they were born. Thus it has been transmitted by Abu Hurayra, may Allah be pleased with him, that the Prophet Muhammad, may Allah bless him and grant him peace, said, 'There is no-one born among the Tribe of Adam who is not touched by *shaytan* at the time of birth – and it is the touch of *shaytan* which makes a child cry when it is born – except for Maryam and her son.' (Al-Bukhari).

Allah also refers to *sayyedina* Zakariyya, his wife Ishba' (Elisabeth), Maryam and *sayyedina* 'Isa in Surat al-Anbiya':

**And (remember) when Zakariyya called to his Lord, 'My Lord, do not leave me without a child – and You are the best of those who grant inheritance.'**

**And We heard his prayer, and We gave him Yahya, and We made his wife fertile – surely they were swift to do good, and they prayed to Us with longing and fear, and they were in awe of Us.**

**And (remember) the one who remained chaste (Maryam), and so We breathed in her of Our Spirit, and made her and her son ('Isa) a sign for all the worlds. (21.89-91).**

It is said that Ishba' the wife of Zakariyya, and Hannah the mother of Maryam, were sisters. It is also said that Ishba' and Maryam were sisters. Allah knows best.

As well as being one of the Prophets who is mentioned by name in the passage from Surat al-An'am which has already been quoted in Chapter Two, *sayyedina* Zakariyya is also referred to again in the *surah* which is named after Maryam, Surah Maryam:

> **(This is) a reminder of the mercy of your Lord to His slave, Zakariyya, when he called to his Lord in secret prayer, saying, 'My Lord, surely my bones have become fragile, and my head shines with grey hair, and my prayers to You, my Lord, have never been in vain, and surely I am concerned about who will succeed me, as my wife is barren – so grant me a successor from Your presence who will inherit from me, and who will inherit from the family of Ya'qub, and make him, my Lord, pleasing (to You).'**
>
> **(It was said to him), 'O Zakariyya, surely We give you good news of a son whose name is Yahya – and We have never given that name to anyone before him.'**
>
> **He said, 'My Lord, how can I have a son when my wife is barren and I have become old and weak?'**
>
> **He replied, 'Just like that – your Lord says, "It is easy for Me, just as I created you in the past, when you were not anything."'**
>
> **He said, 'My Lord, give me a sign.'**
>
> **He replied, 'Your sign shall be that you will not speak to anyone for three nights even though you are well.'**
>
> **Then he came out to his people from the sanctuary and gestured to them to glorify (Allah) in the early morning and at nightfall. (19.1-11).**

It has been transmitted by Abu Hurayra, may Allah be pleased with him, that the Prophet Muhammad, may Allah bless him and grant him peace, said, 'Zakariyya was a carpenter.' (Muslim).

# CHAPTER NINE

# THE PROPHET YAHYA
## peace be on him

As we have just seen, *sayyedina* Yahya was the son of *sayyedina* Zakariyya who was descended from *sayyedina* Sulayman, the son of *sayyedina* Da'ud who was descended from Judah, one of the twelve sons of *sayyedina* Ya'qub – who was otherwise known as Israel, peace be on them. It is clear that *sayyedina* Yahya was the man who is known by the Jews and the Christians as John the Baptist.

As we have already seen, the significance of *sayyedina* Yahya lies in the fact that he was the first to openly proclaim the coming of *sayyedina* 'Isa, and to confirm that he was indeed the Messiah whose coming had been foretold in the original Taurah which had been given to *sayyedina* Musa, peace be on them.

As well as being mentioned in the passages which have been quoted in the previous chapter, and as well as being one of the Prophets who is mentioned by name in the passage from Surat al-An'am which has already been quoted in Chapter Two, the following *ayat* from Surah Maryam also refer to *sayyedina* Yahya:

> **(And it was said to him), 'O Yahya, hold fast to the Book!'**
>
> **And We gave him wisdom when he was a boy, and compassion from Our presence, and purity – and he had *taqwa*, and he was kind to his parents, and he was never tyrannical or rebellious.**
>
> **So peace be on him the day he was born, and the day he died, and the day he will be brought back to life! (19.12-15).**

In referring to this passage, *Qadi* 'Iyad states:

> Allah says, **'We gave him judgement as a child.'** (19.12). The commentators say that Allah gave Yahya knowledge of the Book of Allah while he was still a child. Ma'mar said that he was only two or three years old, (according to what is related by Ibn Hanbal in *Zuhd*, Ibn Abi Hatim in his *Tafsir*, ad-Daylami and al-Hakim). The children asked him, 'Why don't you play with us?' He replied, 'Was I created for playing games?' (*Ash-Shifa'* of *Qadi* 'Iyad: 1.2.10).

And:

> Mujahid said, 'Yahya's food was herbs. He used to weep out of fear of Allah until the tears made ridges in his cheeks. He used to eat with the wild animals to avoid mixing with people.' (Ibn Abi Hatim and Ibn Hanbal in *Zuhd*). (*Ash-Shifa'* of *Qadi* 'Iyad: 1.2.24).

It is said that both *sayyedina* Zakariyya and *sayyedina* Yahya were killed as martyrs by some of the Judahites who did not want to hear what they had to say. Allah knows best.

# Chapter Ten

# The Prophet 'Isa
## peace be on him

As we have just seen, *sayyedina* 'Isa was the son of Maryam, the daughter of 'Imran, who was descended from *sayyedina* Sulayman, the son of *sayyedina* Da'ud who was descended from Judah, one of the twelve sons of *sayyedina* Ya'qub – who was otherwise known as Israel, may the blessings and peace of Allah be on all of them.

There is absolutely no doubt about the fact that *sayyedina* 'Isa was the promised Messiah – descended from the family of *sayyedina* Da'ud, from the family of *sayyedina* Ya'qub, from the family of *sayyedina* Ibrahim through his son *sayyedina* Ishaq – whose coming had been foretold in the original Taurah of *sayyedina* Musa, peace be on all of them:

> **And We indeed gave Musa the Book, and We made a succession of Messengers follow after him, and We gave 'Isa ibn Maryam clear proofs and We helped him with the pure spirit (the angel Jibril).**
>
> **So why is it that whenever a Messenger comes to you with what you yourselves do not want, you become arrogant, rejecting some, and killing some? (2.87).**

And:

> **And We sent 'Isa son of Maryam in their footsteps, confirming what was (revealed) before him in the Taurah; and We gave him the Ingil – in which there was guidance and light – confirming what was (revealed) before it in the Taurah, and a guidance and a warning to those who have *taqwa*. (5.46).**

The story of the miraculous conception and birth of *sayyedina* 'Isa – who is ignored by the Jews and known by the Christians as Jesus, the son of Mary – is related in two different places in the Qur'an:

> **(And remember) when the angels said, 'O Mary, surely Allah gives you good news of a word from Him, whose name is the Messiah, 'Isa son of Maryam, who will be honoured in this world and in the next world, and who will be one of those who are near (to Allah) – and he will speak to people from his cradle and when he is a man, and he will be one of those who are righteous.'**
>
> **She replied, 'My Lord, how can I have a child, when no man has touched me?'**
>
> **He replied, 'Just like that – Allah creates whatever He wants. When He decrees something, then all He says to it is, "Be!" and it is.**
>
> **'And He will teach him the Book, and wisdom, and the Taurah, and the Ingil, and he will be a Messenger to the Tribe of Israel, (saying), "Surely I have come to you with a sign from your Lord – surely I will make the shape of a bird from clay for you, and then breathe into it, and it will become a bird by the permission of Allah; and I will heal him who was born blind and the leper, and I will bring the dead to life by the permission of Allah; and I will tell you what you have had to eat and what you have stored away in your houses – surely in that there is certainly a sign for you, if you are believers.**
>
> **"And (I have come) to confirm what was before me from the Taurah, and to make some of what used to be forbidden for you lawful for you – and I have come to you with a sign from your Lord, so have *taqwa* of Allah and obey me. Surely Allah is my Lord and your Lord, so worship Him – that is the straight path."'**
>
> **And when 'Isa perceived their disbelief, he said, 'Who will be my helpers for Allah?'**

**The disciples replied, 'We are Allah's helpers – we believe in Allah, so bear witness that we are Muslims! O our Lord, we believe in what You have revealed and we follow the Messenger, so record us among those who bear witness.' (3.45-53).**

And:

**And mention Mary in the Book – when she withdrew from her people to a place in the east and chose seclusion from them, then We sent Our spirit (the angel Jibril) to her, and he appeared to her as a perfect man.**

**She said, 'Surely I seek refuge in the Merciful One from you, if you have *taqwa*.'**

**He said, 'Surely I am only a Messenger from your Lord, to give you news of a pure son.'**

**She replied, 'How can I have a son when no man has touched me, and when I have never been immoral?'**

**He said, 'Just like that – your Lord says, "It is easy for Me – and We shall make him a sign for mankind, and a mercy from Us – and it is something which has already been decreed."'**

**And so she conceived him, and she withdrew with him to a place which was far away, and the pains of childbirth drove her to the trunk of a palm tree – she said, 'O would that I had died before this and become nothing, forgotten!'**

**And then it was said to her from below her, 'Do not be sad – your Lord has placed a small stream beneath you, and shake the trunk of the palm tree towards you - you will make fresh ripe dates fall around you. So eat and drink and be comforted. And if you meet any man, then say, "Surely I have made a vow to the Merciful One to fast, and I may not speak to anyone today."'**

**Then she brought him to her people, carrying him.**

**They said, 'O Maryam, you have indeed come with something deceitful! O sister of Harun, your father was not a wicked man, and your mother was never immoral!'**

**Then she pointed to him.**

**They said, 'How can we talk to a baby in his cradle?'**

**He said, 'Surely I am the slave of Allah – He has given me the Book, and He has made me a Prophet, and He has made me blessed wherever I may be, and He has made the prayer and *zakat* obligatory for me as long as I live, and He has made me obedient towards the one who bore me, and He has not made me tyrannical or ungrateful – and peace be on me the day I was born, and the day I die, and the day I shall be brought back to life!'**

**Such was 'Isa son of Maryam – (this is) a statement of the truth about which they are in doubt.**

**It is not how it is for Allah to choose any son – glory be to Him! When He decrees something, then all He says to it is 'Be!' and it is.**

**'And surely Allah is my Lord and your Lord, so worship Him. This is the straight path.'** (19.16-36).

In referring to the miraculous birth of *sayyedina* 'Isa, peace be on him, *Qadi* 'Iyad states:

> The Prophet, may Allah bless him and grant him peace, said, "Isa was protected from his touch. *Shaytan* came to thrust his hand on his hip when he was born, attacking the veil.' (Al-Bukhari and Muslim, from Abu Hurayra. The 'veil' either means the placenta or a special veil with which Allah veiled 'Isa.). (*Ash-Shifa'* of *Qadi* 'Iyad: 3.1.4).

As has already been stated in Chapter Eight, it is said that it was because of Hannah's prayer for Maryam and her offspring that *shaytan* could not touch either her or *sayyedina* 'Isa when they were born. Thus it has been transmitted by Abu Hurayra, may Allah be pleased with him, that the Prophet Muhammad, may Allah bless him and grant him peace, said, 'There is no-one born among the Tribe of Adam who is not touched by *shaytan* at the time of birth – and it is the touch of *shaytan* which makes a child cry when it is born – except for Maryam and her son.' (Al-Bukhari).

The place where *sayyedina* 'Isa was born, peace be on him, is also mentioned in one other *ayah* in the Qur'an:

> **And We made a sign of the son of Maryam and his mother, and We gave them a place of refuge in a high place, where there was safety and running water. (23.50).**

It is also said that this *ayah* refers to the place where Maryam and *sayyedina* 'Isa took refuge after his birth, and after they had been forced to leave Jerusalem and flee to Egypt, where they stayed during the early part of *sayyedina* 'Isa's childhood. Allah knows best.

*Sayyedina* 'Isa's childhood and early manhood, and his return to Jerusalem from Egypt with his mother, are not mentioned in the Qur'an, but there are several references to what happened once he began to call the Tribe of Israel to only worship Allah and to follow the teachings of *sayyedina* Musa which were in the Taurah. The following *ayat*, for example, refer to the response of the men who became *sayyedina* 'Isa's disciples:

> **O you who believe, be Allah' helpers, just as when 'Isa son of Maryam said to the disciples, 'Who will be my helpers for Allah?' and the disciples replied, 'We are Allah's helpers.' And a party of the Tribe of Israel believed, and a party disbelieved, and We strengthened those who believed against their enemy, and so they became the ones who prevailed. (61.14).**

The conflict between those who accepted *sayyedina* 'Isa and those who rejected him, peace be on him, often focused around his extraordinary miracles, which he always attributed to Allah and not to himself. It is not surprising, in view of these miracles, that some of those who accepted *sayyedina* 'Isa did so rather too enthusiastically, and in so doing mistakenly considered him to be the 'son' of God, thereby idolising him and making him an object of worship. Allah refers to this misconception in the following passage from Surat al-Ma'ida, which refers to Allah's questioning all His Messengers on the Last Day:

**On the Day when Allah will gather all the Messengers together and will say, 'What was the response to you?' they will say, 'We do not know – surely it is only You Who knows what is hidden.'**

**And Allah will say, 'O 'Isa son of Maryam, remember My blessing on you and on your mother – how I strengthened you with the pure spirit (the angel Jibril), so that you spoke to people from the cradle and as a man; and how I taught you the Book, and wisdom and the Taurah and the Ingil; and how you made the shape of a bird from clay by My permission, and then breathed into it, so that it became a bird by My permission; and how you healed him who was born blind and the leper by My permission; and how you raised the dead by My permission; and how I restrained the Tribe of Israel from harming you when you came to them with clear proofs, and those of them who disbelieved said, "Surely this is nothing but magic!"**

**'And (remember) when I inspired the disciples to, "Believe in Me and in My Messenger," and they said, "We believe, so bear witness that we are Muslims!"'**

**And (remember) when the disciples said, 'O 'Isa son of Maryam, is your Lord able to send down a table from heaven for us?'**

**He replied, 'Have *taqwa* of Allah if you are believers!'**

**They said, 'We want to eat from it, and put our hearts at ease, and know that you have told us the truth, and be among those who witness it.'**

**'Isa son of Maryam said, 'O Allah, our Lord, send down a table from heaven for us with a feast for us, for the first of us and the last of us, and as a sign from You, and provide for us – and You are the Best of those who provide.'**

**Allah said, 'Surely I will send it down for you – and if any of you disbelieves afterwards, then I will surely punish him with a punishment with which I have never punished anyone else in all the worlds before!'**

(It is said that this feast replenished itself as long as no one stored up any of it for the next day, and that as soon as someone did this, it disappeared. Allah knows best.)

**And when Allah says, 'O 'Isa son of Maryam, did you say to people, "Take me and my mother as two gods instead of Allah,"?' he will reply, 'Glory be to You – it was not for me to say what I had no right to say! If I ever said that, then You would certainly know it. You know what is in me, and I do not know what is in You – surely it is only You Who knows what is hidden. I only told them what You commanded me – to, "Worship Allah, my Lord and your Lord," and while I dwelt among them I was a watcher over them, and when You took me up, then You were a Watcher over them – and You watch over everything.**

**'If You punish them, then surely they are Your slaves, and if You forgive them, then surely You are the Mighty, the Wise.'**

**Allah will say, 'This is a Day when the truthful will benefit from their truthfulness, for gardens underneath which rivers flow will be theirs, dwelling there for ever – Allah is pleased with them and they are pleased with Him – that is the great success.'**

**The dominion of the heavens and the earth and whatever is in them belongs to Allah – and He has power over everything. (5.109-120).**

Elsewhere in the Qur'an, Allah makes it perfectly clear that both *sayyedina* 'Isa and Maryam were only human beings:

**The Messiah son of Maryam was only a Messenger, like the Messengers who went before him, and his mother was a truthful woman, and they both used to eat food.**

**See how We clarify the signs for them – and then see how they make up lies!**

**Say: 'Do you worship what does not have any power to either harm or benefit you, instead of Allah?'**

**And it is Allah Who is the One Who Hears, the One Who Knows. (5.75-76).**

And:

**Allah has struck a metaphor of those who disbelieve: the wife of Nuh and the wife of Lut – who were under two of Our slaves from among Our righteous slaves, and yet they betrayed them, so that they (Nuh and Lut) were unable to be of any use to them at all against Allah, and it was said to them: 'Enter into the Fire along with those who enter it.'**

**And Allah has struck a metaphor of those who believe: the wife of Firaoun, when she said, 'My Lord, prepare a home for me with You in the Garden, and deliver me from Firaoun and his actions, and deliver me from people who are wrong doers.**

**And Maryam the daughter of 'Imran, who preserved her chastity, and so We breathed in it of Our Spirit – and she confirmed the words of her Lord and His Books, and she was one of those who are obedient. (66.10-12).**

It has been transmitted by Abu Musa al-Ash'ari, may Allah be pleased with him, that the Prophet Muhammad, may Allah bless him and grant him peace, said, 'Many men have reached perfection, but few women have reached perfection, except Asiyya the wife of Firaoun, and Maryam the daughter of 'Imran.' (Al-Bukhari).

It follows that anyone who thinks – by virtue of Maryam's degree of perfection, and by virtue of the miraculous nature of the immaculate conception – that *sayyedina* 'Isa can somehow be associated with being God in any way is mistaken:

> **Those who say, 'Surely Allah is the Messiah, son of Maryam,' have indeed disbelieved.**
>
> **Say: 'And who would have any power at all over Allah if He wished to destroy the Messiah son of Maryam, and his mother, and whoever is on earth, all together? And dominion over the heavens and the earth and what is between them belongs to Allah – He creates what He wants – and Allah has power over everything. (5.17).**

It also follows that the concept of a Trinity is false:

> **O People of the Book, do not go to extremes in your religion, and do not say anything about Allah except the truth.**
>
> **Surely the Messiah 'Isa son of Maryam was a Messenger of Allah, and His Word which He sent down into Maryam, and a Spirit from Him – so believe in Allah and His Messengers, and do not say, 'Three.' Stop it! (That would be) better for you. Surely Allah is only One God! Glory be to Him – far beyond His having a son – when whatever is in the heavens and whatever is in the earth is His. And Allah is enough to look after it.**
>
> **The Messiah would never be too proud to be a slave of Allah, and neither would the angels who are near (to Allah) – and as for whoever is too proud to be His slave, and is arrogant, He will gather them altogether to Him.**

**And as for those who believed and did good, He will give them their reward in full, and increase it for them out of His generosity – and as for those who were proud and arrogant, He will punish them with a painful punishment, and they will not find anyone to be their friend or helper instead of Allah. (4.171-173).**

And:

**Those who say, 'Surely Allah is the Messiah, son of Mary,' are certainly disbelievers.**

**And the Messiah said: 'O Tribe of Israel, worship Allah, my Lord and your Lord. As for whoever associates partners with Allah, surely Allah has certainly forbidden him the Garden and his abode will be the Fire – and for the wrong doers there will be no helpers.'**

**Those who say, 'Surely Allah is one of three in a trinity,' are certainly disbelievers – for there is no god except the One God. And if they do not desist from what they are saying, a painful punishment will certainly befall those of them who disbelieve.**

**Will they not rather turn to Allah in repentance and seek His forgiveness? And Allah is Forgiving, Compassionate.**

**The Messiah son of Maryam was only a Messenger, like the Messengers who went before him, and his mother was a truthful woman, and they both used to eat food.**

**See how We clarify the signs for them – and then see how they make up lies! (5.72-75).**

As well as being one of the Prophets who is mentioned by name in the passages from Surat an-Nisa and Surat al-An'am which have already been quoted in Chapter Two, *sayyedina* 'Isa is also referred to in this *ayah* from Surat al-Baqara, in which Allah indicates that although some of His Messengers were more blessed than others, this does not mean that they were not human beings:

**And of these Messengers We have made some to excel others: among them are those to whom Allah spoke, and among them are those whom He exalted in degree above others; and We gave 'Isa son of Maryam clear signs and strengthened him with the pure spirit (the angel Jibril). And if Allah had wanted, those who came after them would not have fought with each other, after the clear signs that had come to them – but they differed, and from among them were those who believed, and from among them were those who disbelieved; and if Allah had wanted, they would not have fought with each other, but Allah does what He wants. (2.253)**

Thus in spite of his extraordinary purity, and the piercing clarity of his words and signs, there were inevitably people who rejected *sayyedina* 'Isa, both while he was on earth and after he had been taken away from it:

**And when the son of Maryam is given as an example your people turn away from it and say, 'Are our gods better, or him?' And they only mention him for the sake of argument – indeed, they are an argumentative people! Surely he was only a slave whom We blessed, and whom We gave as an example to the Tribe of Israel.**

**And if We had wanted, We could certainly have put angels among you to be *khalifs* in the earth; and surely there is certainly knowledge about the Hour, so do not be in any doubt about it, and follow Me – that is the straight path; and do not let *shaytan* lead you astray – surely he is clearly your enemy.**

**And when 'Isa came with clear proofs, he said, 'I have indeed come to you with wisdom and in order to clarify what you used to disagree about for you – so have *taqwa* of Allah and obey me. Surely it is Allah Who is my Lord and your Lord, so worship Him – that is the straight path.**

**But the groups among them disagreed – so woe to those who do wrong, from the punishment of a painful Day. (43.57-65).**

And:

> **And We certainly sent Nuh and Ibrahim, and placed the prophethood and the Book among their descendants: among them is he who is rightly guided, and many of them are evil-livers.**
>
> **Then We made Our Messengers follow in their footsteps, and We made 'Isa son of Maryam follow on, and We gave him the Ingil, and We placed compassion and mercy in the hearts of those who followed him; and it was they who invented monasticism – We did not ordain it for them – only seeking the pleasure of Allah, but they did not observe it with true observance.**
>
> **So We give those of them who believe their reward, and many of them are evil-livers. (57.26-27).**

There is no known copy of the original revelation which was given to *sayyedina* 'Isa, peace be on him – the Ingil – in existence today, which perhaps partly explains why his teachings have been rewritten and redefined so often during the last two millennia. According to the *Gospel of Barnabas,* the Ingil was never actually contained in a written form – being more like a well of wisdom in *sayyedina* 'Isa's heart from which he drew when it was needed – but it is clear that as well as speaking Aramaic, *sayyedina* 'Isa also knew Hebrew, since his purpose was to re-establish the original teachings of Musa among the Tribe of Israel, in accordance with the Taurah, which was written in ancient Hebrew, and which had already been so significantly changed and corrupted by the time of his miraculous birth, that he was in fact rejected by the very Jewish priesthood who claimed to be the rightful custodians of *sayyedina* Musa's teachings!

Indeed, perhaps one of the main reasons why the Jewish priesthood opposed *sayyedina* 'Isa and wished to have him killed was because he knew exactly which parts of the Taurah which had originally been revealed to *sayyedina* Musa had been subsequently changed by the Jews, having been given direct knowledge of the original Taurah by Allah.

*Sayyedina* 'Isa was also most probably equally aware of the distortions and amendments contained in the additional books which had been written *after* the death of *sayyedina* Musa, and which purported to faithfully record the history of the Tribe of Israel thereafter.

In other words, with the coming of *sayyedina* 'Isa, all the misrepresentations and changes to the original teachings of *sayyedina* Musa which had gradually been introduced by the Jewish priesthood during the nine centuries that had elapsed after the reign of *sayyedina* Sulayman had come to an end were suddenly in grave danger of being exposed, and their hierarchy of being destroyed. This is why they rejected *sayyedina* 'Isa, peace be on him, and this is why they plotted with the Romans to have him killed. Although *sayyedina* Zakariyya and *sayyedina* Yahya, peace be on them, were probably martyred by some of those among the Tribe of Israel who rejected them, Allah makes it clear that they did not kill *sayyedina* 'Isa, peace be on him, even though it was their intention to do so:

> **And they plotted, and Allah plotted – and Allah is the best of plotters.**
>
> **(And remember) when Allah said, 'O 'Isa, surely I am going to take you up, and raise you up to Me, and free you from those who disbelieve – and I will put those who follow you above those who disbelieve until the Day of Standing – and then you will all return to Me, and I will judge between you concerning what you used to disagree about.**
>
> **'And as for those who disbelieve, I shall punish them with an intense punishment in this world and in the next world – and they will not have any helpers.**
>
> **'And as for those who believe and do good, He will give them their reward in full – and Allah does not love wrong doers.**
>
> **'And what We are telling you is from among the signs, and a wise reminder.'**

> **Surely the similarity of 'Isa with Allah is like the similarity of Adam. He created him from dust, and then said to him, 'Be!' – and he is.**
>
> **This is the truth from your Lord, so do not be one of those who doubt.**
>
> **And as for whoever argues with you about him ('Isa), after the knowledge which has come to you, then say: 'Come, let us summon our sons and your sons, and our women and your women, and ourselves and yourselves, and then let us humbly pray, and invoke the curse of Allah upon those who lie.'**
>
> **Surely this explanation is certainly true, and there is not any god except Allah – and surely Allah is certainly the Mighty, the Wise. And if they turn away, then surely Allah is aware of those who are corrupt. (3.54-63).**

Allah also refers to the fact that *sayyedina* 'Isa was neither killed nor crucified in the following passage from Surat an-Nisa, in which He describes the consequences of the actions of those from among the Tribe of Israel who disbelieved and broke their covenant with Allah:

> **And because of their breaking their covenant, and their rejecting the signs of Allah, and their killing the Prophets without any justification, and their saying, 'Our hearts are covered over,'– indeed Allah has set a seal on them because of their disbelief, so that they will not believe except for a few – and because of their disbelief and their spreading a great slander against Maryam, and their saying, 'Surely we killed the Messiah, 'Isa son of Maryam', a Messenger of Allah –**
>
> **And they did not kill him and they did not crucify him, but it appeared so to them. And surely those who disagree about it are certainly in doubt about it – they have no knowledge about it except that they follow speculation. And they did not kill him for certain – but Allah took him up to Himself. And Allah was ever Mighty, Wise.**

> **And there is not one of the People of the Book but will certainly believe in him before his death – and on the Day of Standing he will be a witness against them.**
>
> **– And because of the wrong doing of the Jews, We forbade them the good things which were permitted for them (before), and because of their turning away from the way of Allah so much, and their taking usury – and they were indeed forbidden it – and their devouring people's wealth through deception, We have prepared a painful punishment for those of them who disbelieve.**
>
> **But those of them who are firm in knowledge, and the believers, believe in what has been revealed to you (Muhammad), and in what has been revealed before you – and those who establish the prayer, and those who pay the *zakat*, and those who believe in Allah and the Last Day – to these we shall give a great reward. (4.155-162).**

According to the *Gospel of Barnabas,* it was Judas Iscariot who was arrested and subsequently crucified by the Roman soldiers who mistakenly thought him to be *sayyedina* 'Isa. Although none of today's officially accepted Gospels – or the *Gospel of Barnabas* or any other Gospel for that matter – are capable of being authenticated (instead it is simply claimed that they are 'divinely inspired'), the following references to the *Gospel of Barnabas* which are to be found in *Jesus, Prophet of Islam* by Muhammad 'Ata'ur-Rahim are of interest, since they do at least explore this possibility and its consequences:

> In the account given by Barnabas, we are told that at the time of the arrest, Judas was transformed by the Creator so that even his mother and his closest followers believed him to be Jesus. It was not until Jesus appeared to them, after his supposed death, that they were informed of what had really happened. This would explain why there is such confusion surrounding the events which took place at this time, and why some accounts, written by people who were not present at those events, support the mistaken belief that it was Jesus who was crucified.

And:

> Plotinus, who lived in the fourth century, tells us that he had read a book called *The Journeys of the Apostles* which related the acts of Peter, John, Andrew, Thomas and Paul. Among other things, it stated that Jesus was not crucified, but another in his place, and therefore he laughed at those who believed that they had crucified him.

And:

> There is no other known historical record of what happened to Jesus after the 'crucifixion' other than in the *Gospel of Barnabas* and the Qur'an. These both describe the event which is generally known as the 'ascension' in the four accepted Gospels, in which Jesus was taken away from this world.

Although there is no record of the original Ingil ever having existed in a written form, in the original Aramaic, many of *sayyedina* 'Isa's followers, and the followers of his followers, did write accounts of what he had said and done. These accounts came to be called 'the gospels'. At one time there were at least three hundred of these gospels, but many of them were suppressed and destroyed both by the Romans and by the Jews, who regarded the teachings of *sayyedina* 'Isa as a threat to the security of their own power elites and structures.

During the first three centuries after the disappearance of *sayyedina* 'Isa, his early followers were constantly harassed and persecuted wherever they went – which resulted in his teachings being spread far and wide, as his followers travelled further afield in search of safety, taking their newly acquired knowledge with them. It was when some aspects of the teachings of *sayyedina* 'Isa were conveyed to people in Greece and Italy who did not belong to the Tribe of Israel – especially by Paul of Tarsus who was a reformed Jew who had never even met *sayyedina* 'Isa – that a split occurred in the early church, between the two groups who in time were to become known as the Unitarians and the Trinitarians, with each group calling the other heretics.

Although, at this stage, the doctrine of Trinity had not yet been formulated, it was Paul who prepared the intellectual way for it, for he claimed to have met *sayyedina* 'Isa in a vision on the road to Damascus and stated that there was now a new covenant, and that whoever believed in *sayyedina* 'Isa was no longer obliged to follow the *shari'a* of *sayyedina* Musa which, it will be remembered, *sayyedina* 'Isa had originally come to uphold and re-establish among the Tribe of Israel. Paul emphasised that it was enough to believe in *sayyedina* 'Isa in order to have all one's sins in this world forgiven and to gain everlasting salvation in the next world.

These twin doctrines of the new covenant and of the atonement and forgiveness of sins, based firmly on the mistaken belief that it was *sayyedina* 'Isa who had been crucified, gained increasing popularity among both the Greeks and the Romans, although needless to say they were rejected by the true followers of *sayyedina* 'Isa, and especially by those who had been his close companions, including Barnabas, who preferred to hold to what he, peace be on him, had personally taught them.

It was not until the teachings of *sayyedina* 'Isa had been sufficiently redefined and harnessed by the Romans – so that these teachings no longer threatened to destroy their Empire, but rather began to serve as a means of binding the Roman Empire together – that what has become known as 'the New Testament' began to take on the form which it has today.

It was not until the Council of Nicea in 325 CE that the Roman Emperor Constantine – who at the time claimed to be 'neutral' on the grounds that he was not a Christian – decided that the Paulinian version of Christianity represented the true teachings of *sayyedina* 'Isa, and that the gospels of Mathew, Mark, Luke and John should become the officially accepted gospels, and that all other gospels, including the *Gospel of Barnabas*, were to be destroyed – along with those who were found to have them in their possession – a decision which resulted in many of the early gospels being lost for good, and millions of Unitarian Christians being martyred in the years that followed.

It was also at the Council of Nicea, after over two centuries of debate, that *sayyedina* 'Isa was officially granted divine status, and with the official instatement at the Council of Constantinople in 381 CE of 'the Holy Ghost' as the 'third person', the doctrine of Trinity which had begun to emerge during the intervening period finally came of age, some three and a half centuries after the disappearance of *sayyedina* 'Isa.

Shortly after the Council of Constantinople, the Roman Emperor Theodosius made it a capital offence to reject the doctrine of Trinity, thereby laying the foundations for the Mediaeval and Spanish Inquisitions which were to flourish centuries later – by which time the doctrines of the new covenant, and of the atonement and forgiveness of sins, and of the trinity, had become so deeply embedded in the Christian psyche that no amount of reformations, ancient or modern, and however well-intentioned, could dislodge them.

There are many accounts – some of which are more reliable and authentic than others – of some of the miraculous events which characterised the relatively short time spent by *sayyedina* 'Isa in this world. Whereas the accounts which are contained in the officially accepted Gospels are relatively well-known, the accounts which are to be found both in the *Gospel of Barnabas* (which has somehow survived all attempts to destroy it) and in the *hadith* collections of the Muslims are not.

The following extract from the *Gospel of Barnabas*, for example, (which is taken from the translation of Lonsdale and Laura Ragg) describes what is alleged to have taken place immediately before the miraculous feeding of the five thousand – an account which, as well as furnishing an explanation as to why such a large crowd had gathered in the first place, cannot be found in the four officially accepted Gospels, and for obvious reasons, since it describes how *sayyedina* 'Isa publicly demonstrated that he could not possibly be identified with God, simply by comparing his human attributes with God's divine attributes:

> Accordingly the governor and the priest and the king prayed Jesus that in order to quiet the people he should mount

up into a lofty place and speak to the people. Then went up Jesus on to one of the twelve stones which Joshua made the twelve tribes take up from the midst of Jordan, when all Israel passed over there dry shod; and he said with a loud voice: 'Let our priest go up into a high place whence he may confirm my words.'

Thereupon the priest went up thither; to whom Jesus said distinctly, so that everyone might hear: 'It is written in the testament and covenant of the living God that our God has no beginning; neither shall He ever have an end.'

The priest answered: 'Even so it is written therein.'

Jesus said: 'It is written there that our God by His word alone has created all things.'

'Even so it is,' said the priest.

Jesus said: 'It is written there that God is invisible and hidden from the mind of man, seeing He is incorporeal and uncomposed, without variableness.'

'So it is truly,' said the priest.

Jesus said: 'It is written there how that the heaven of heavens cannot contain Him, seeing that our God is infinite.'

'So said Solomon the Prophet,' said the priest, 'O Jesus.'

Said Jesus: 'It is written there that God has no need forasmuch as He eats not, sleeps not, and suffers not from any deficiency.'

'So is it,' said the priest.

Said Jesus: 'It is written there that our God is everywhere, and that there is not any other god but He, Who strikes down and makes whole, and does all that pleases Him.'

'So it is written,' replied the priest.

Then Jesus, having lifted up his hands, said: 'Lord our God, this is my faith wherewith I shall come to Your judgement: in testimony against every one that shall believe the contrary.'

And turning himself towards the people, he said, 'Repent, for from all that of which the priest has said that it is written in the book of Moses, the covenant of God for ever, you may perceive your sin; for that I am a visible man and a morsel of clay that walks upon the earth, mortal as are other men. And I have had a beginning, and shall have an end, and am such that I cannot create a fly over again.' (*The Gospel of Barnabas*: 95).

Unlike the officially accepted Gospels of the New Testament – and indeed the *Gospel of Barnabas* or any other Gospel for that matter – which purport to record some of the actions and words of *sayyedina* 'Isa, peace be on him, a *hadith* which records the words or actions of the Prophet Muhammad, may Allah bless him and grant him peace, is not accepted as reliable unless, as we have already seen in the *Foreword*, it can be traced back through a chain of transmission made up of reliable people, from person to person, back to someone who was a companion of the Prophet Muhammad, may Allah bless him and grant him peace, and who actually witnessed the event or heard the words to which the *hadith* relates.

Accordingly any quotations concerning *sayyedina* 'Isa from any of the Gospels, or from any other ancient source, cannot be given the same weight or accepted with the same confidence as a reliable, fully authenticated *hadith*, no matter how compelling its words may be – although of course sometimes the truth of what is said is so self-evident that it cannot be ignored. This is probably particularly true of those traditions which were transmitted by the very early Unitarian followers of Jesus whose descendants eventually embraced Islam during the 7th and 8th centuries CE.

For as well as those *hadith* of the Prophet Muhammad which refer specifically to *sayyedina* 'Isa, may the blessings and peace of Allah be on them, there are also many other Muslim traditions which give accounts of the sayings and deeds of *sayyedina* 'Isa. These traditions were originally gathered together by the early followers of *sayyedina* 'Isa, especially those early Unitarian followers who spread to Arabia and North Africa. When the Prophet Muhammad, may Allah bless him and grant him peace, came, many of the followers of these followers embraced Islam. They had retained these traditions about *sayyedina* 'Isa, peace be on him, and had passed them down from generation to generation.

Many of these traditions subsequently found their way into Ath-Thalabi's *Stories of the Prophets*. The following selection of these traditions is taken from the selection which appears in *Jesus, Prophet of Islam* by Muhammad 'Ata'ur-Rahim:

Jesus, son of Mary, peace be upon him, said, 'The world consists of three days: yesterday which has passed, from which you have nothing in your hand; tomorrow of which you do not know whether you will reach it or not; and today in which you are, so avail yourself of it.'

And he said also, 'The world is both seeking and sought. He who seeks the next world, this world seeks him until his provision in it is complete; and he who seeks the present world, the next world seeks him until death comes and seizes him by the neck.'

Jesus, peace be upon him, said, 'He who seeks after the world is like one who drinks sea water; the more he drinks, the more his thirst increases, until it kills him.'

It is related that Jesus, peace be upon him, passed three people whose bodies were wasted and who were pale and said, 'What has brought on you that which I see?' They replied, 'Fear of the Fire.' He said, 'It is Allah's duty to render secure him who fears.' Afterwards he passed from them and came to another three, and lo, they were in greater emaciation and paleness, so he said, 'What has brought on you that which I see?' They replied, 'Desire for the Garden.' He said, 'It is Allah's duty to give you what you hope for.' After that he passed from them and came to another three, and lo, they were in still greater emaciation and paleness as though mirrors of light were over their faces, so he said, 'What has brought on you that which I see?' They replied, 'We love Allah, Great and Glorious is He.' He said, 'You are those who are nearest to Allah; you are those who are nearest to Allah; you are those who are nearest to Allah.'

The following is related on the authority of Jabir, on the authority of Laith:

A man accompanied Jesus, son of Mary, peace be upon him, and said, 'I will be with you and will accompany you.' So they set off and came to the bank of a river and sat down to breakfast; and they had three loaves. They ate two loaves, and a third loaf was left over. Then Jesus, peace be upon him, rose up and went to the river and drank, after which he returned, but did not find the loaf; so he said to the man, 'Who took the loaf?' He replied, 'I do not know.'

Then he set off with his companion and saw a gazelle with two of her young. The narrator said: he called one of them and it came to him; then he cut its throat and roasted part of it, and he and that man ate. Then he said to the young gazelle, 'Rise, by the permission of Allah.' When it arose and went away, he said to the man, 'I ask you by Him Who has shown you this sign, who took the loaf?' He replied, 'I do not know.'

Afterwards they came to a wadi with water in it and Jesus took the man's hand and they walked on the water. Then, when they had crossed, he said to him, 'I ask you by Him Who has shown you this sign, who took the loaf?' He replied, 'I do not know.'

Then they came to a desert and sat down, and Jesus, peace be upon him, began to collect earth and a heap of sand, after which he said, 'Become gold, by the permission of Allah, Exalted be He!' It became gold, and he divided it into three parts and said, 'A third is for me, a third for you, and a third for him who took the loaf.' Then he said, 'I am the one who took the loaf.' He said, 'It is all yours.'

Jesus, peace be upon him, then left him, and two men came to him in the desert while he had the wealth with him and wished to take it from him and kill him. He said, 'It is among us in thirds; so send one of you to the village to buy food for us to eat.'

The narrator said: they sent one of them, and he who was sent said to himself, 'Why should I divide this wealth with these men? I shall put poison in this food and kill them and take the wealth myself.' So he did so. And these two men said, 'Why should we give this man a third of the wealth? When he returns we shall kill him, and divide the wealth between us.'

The narrator said: so when he returned they killed him and ate the food and died; and that wealth remained in the desert with those three men lying dead beside it. Then Jesus, peace be upon him, passed them in that condition and said to his companions, 'This is the world, so beware of it.'

The disciples said to Jesus, peace be upon him, 'How is it that you can walk on water and we cannot?' Then he said to them, 'What do you think of the *dinar* and the *dirham*?' (pieces of money). They replied, 'They are good.' He said, 'But they and mud are alike to me.'

Jesus, the Messiah, peace be upon him, used to take nothing with him but a comb and a jug. Then he saw a man combing his beard with his fingers, so he threw away the comb; and he saw another drinking from a river with the palms of his hands, so he threw away the jug.

Obaid, son of 'Omar, said, 'The Messiah, son of Mary, peace be upon him, used to wear hair clothing, and eat wild fruits, and he had no son to die, and no house to be demolished, and he stored up nothing for the morrow. He slept wherever the evening overtook him.'

If you wish, you may follow him who was the Spirit and the Word, Jesus, son of Mary, peace be upon him, for he used to say, 'My seasoning is hunger, my under-garment is fear of Allah, my outer-garment is wool, my fire in winter is the rays of the sun, my lamp is the moon, my riding beast is my feet, and my food and fruit are what the earth brings forth (i.e. without cultivation). At night I have nothing and in the morning I have nothing, yet there is no one on earth richer than I.'

Jesus, son of Mary, peace be upon him, said, 'In the last days there will be learned men who teach abstinence in the world but will not be abstinent themselves, who will teach men to take delight in the next world but will not take delight in it themselves, and who will warn men against coming before rulers but will not refrain themselves. They will draw near to the rich and keep far from the poor; they will be pleasant to great men but will shrink from humble men. Those are the brethren of the devils and the enemies of the Merciful.'

Ka'b al-Akbar said, 'Jesus, son of Mary, was a ruddy man, inclined to white; he did not have long hair, and he never

> anointed his head. Jesus used to walk barefoot, and he took no house, or adornment, or goods, or clothes, or provision, except his day's food. Wherever the sun set, he arranged his feet in prayer till the morning came. He was curing the blind from birth, and the leper, and raising the dead by Allah's permission, and was telling his people what they were eating in their houses and what they were storing up for the morrow, and he was walking on the surface of the water in the sea. His head was dishevelled and his face was small; he was an ascetic in the world, longing for the next world and eager for the worship of Allah. He was a pilgrim in the earth till the Jews sought him and desired to kill him. Then Allah raised him up to heaven; and Allah knows best.' (*Jesus, Prophet of Islam*: 10).

One of the Prophets whom the Prophet Muhammad met on the *'isra' wa'l-mi'raj* – his miraculous night journey through the seven heavens and then past the limit of forms to the Presence of Allah – was *sayyedina* 'Isa, may the blessings and peace of Allah be on them. Thus we know that for the time being at least, *sayyedina* 'Isa is in one of the seven heavens, in the Unseen, and as yet has not experienced death.

The Prophet Muhammad, may the blessings and peace of Allah be on him, also confirmed that towards the end of time, *sayyedina* 'Isa would return to this world in order to destroy the Antichrist – who is called the *Dajjal* by the Muslims – and his followers, and that after this had occurred, the *deen* of Islam would be established throughout the world:

> It has been related by Ibn Mas'ud, may Allah be pleased with him, that the Prophet Muhammad, may Allah bless him and grant him peace, said, 'On the night of the *'isra'* (night journey), I met my father Abraham, Moses and Jesus, and they discussed the Hour. The matter was referred first to Abraham, then to Moses, and both said, "I have no knowledge of it." Then it was referred to Jesus, who said, "No-one knows about its timing except Allah; what my Lord told me was that the Dajjal will appear, and when he sees me he will begin to melt like lead. Allah will destroy him when he sees

me. The Muslims will fight against the *kafirs*, and even the trees and rocks will say, 'O Muslim, there is a *kafir* hiding behind me – come and kill him!' Allah will destroy the *kafirs*, and the people will return to their own lands. Then Gog and Magog will appear from all directions, eating and drinking everything they find. The people will complain to me, so I will pray to Allah and He will destroy them, so that the earth will be filled with their stench. Allah will send rain which will wash their bodies into the sea. My Lord has told me that when that happens, the Hour will be very close, like a pregnant woman whose time is due, but her family do not know exactly when she will deliver."' (Ahmad ibn Hanbal: Musnad, 1.375).

These events are described in greater detail in the following *hadith*:

An-Nuwas ibn Sam'an said, 'One morning the Prophet, may Allah bless him and grant him peace, spoke about the Dajjal. Sometimes he described him as insignificant, and sometimes he described him as so dangerous that we thought he was in the clump of date-palms nearby. When we went to him later on, he noticed that fear in our faces, and asked, "What is the matter with you?" We said, "O Messenger of Allah, this morning you spoke of the Dajjal; sometimes you described him as insignificant, and sometimes you described him as being so dangerous that we thought he was in the clump of date-palms nearby."

'The Prophet, may Allah bless him and grant him peace, said, "I fear for you in other matters besides the Dajjal. If he appears whilst I am among you, I will contend with him on your behalf. But if he appears while I am not among you, then each man must contend with him on his own behalf, and Allah will take care of every Muslim on my behalf. The Dajjal will be a young man, with short, curly hair, and one eye floating. I would liken him to Abdal-'Uzza ibn Qatan. Whoever amongst you lives to see him should recite the opening *ayat* of Surat al-Kahf. He will appear on the way between Syria and Iraq, and will create disaster left and right. O servants of Allah, adhere to the Path of Truth."

'We said, "O Messenger of Allah, how long will he stay on the earth?" He said, "For forty days, one day like a year, and one day like a month, and one day like a week, and the rest of the days will be like your days.'

'We said, "O Messenger of Allah, for the day which is like a year, will one day's prayers be sufficient?" He said, "No, you must make an estimate of the time, and then observe the prayers."

'We asked, "O Messenger of Allah, how quickly will he walk upon the earth?" He said, "Like a cloud driven by the wind. He will come to the people and call them (to a false religion), and they will believe in him and respond to him. He will issue a command to the sky, and it will rain; and to the earth, and it will produce crops. After grazing on these crops, their animals will return with their udders full of milk and their flanks stretched. Then he will come to another people and will call them (to a false religion), but they will reject his call. He will depart from them; they will suffer famine and will possess nothing in the form of wealth. Then he will pass through the wasteland and will say, 'Bring forth your treasures', and the treasures will come forth, like swarms of bees. Then he will call a man brimming with youth; he will strike him with a sword and cut him in two, then place the two pieces at the distance between an archer and his target. Then he will call him, and the young man will come running and laughing.

'"At that point, Allah will send the Messiah, son of Mary, and he will descend to the white minaret in the east of Damascus, wearing two garments dyed with saffron, placing his hands on the wings of two angels. When he lowers his head, beads of perspiration will fall from it, and when he raises his head, beads like pearls will scatter from it. Every *kafir* who smells his fragrance will die, and his breath will reach as far as he can see. He will search for the Dajjal until he finds him at the gate of Ludd (the biblical Lydda, now known as Lod), where he will kill him.

'"Then a people whom Allah has protected will come to Jesus son of Mary, and he will wipe their faces (i.e. wipe the traces of hardship from their faces) and tell them of their status in Paradise. At that time Allah will reveal to Jesus: 'I

> have brought forth some of My servants whom no-one will be able to fight. Take My servants safely to at-Tur.'
>
> '"Then Allah will send Gog and Magog, and they will swarm down from every slope. The first of them will pass by the Lake of Tiberias, and will drink some of its water; the last of them will pass by it and say, 'There used to be water here'. Jesus, the Prophet of Allah, and his Companions will be besieged until a bull's head will be dearer to them than one hundred dinars are to you nowadays.
>
> '"Then Jesus and his Companions will pray to Allah, and He will send insects who will bite the people of Gog and Magog on their necks, so that in the morning they will all perish as one. Then Jesus and his Companions will come down and will not find any nook or cranny on earth which is free from their putrid stench. Jesus and his Companions will again pray to Allah, Who will send birds like the necks of camels; they will seize the bodies of Gog and Magog and throw them wherever Allah wills. Then Allah will send rain which no house or tent will be able to keep out, and the earth will be cleansed, until it will look like a mirror. Then the earth will be told to bring forth its fruit and restore its blessing.
>
> On that day, a group of people will be able to eat from a single pomegranate and seek shelter under its skin (i.e. the fruit will be so large). A milch-camel will give so much milk that a whole party will be able to drink from it; a cow will give so much milk that a whole tribe will be able to drink from it; and a milch-sheep will give so much milk that a whole family will be able to drink from it.
>
> At that time, Allah will send a pleasant wind which will soothe them even under their armpits, and will take the soul of every Muslim. Only the most wicked people will be left, and they will fornicate like asses; then the Last Hour will come upon them."'(Sahih Muslim, *Kitab al-Fitan wa Ashrat as-Sa'ah*, 8.196-199).

The Prophet Muhammad also confirmed that after the Dajjal and his followers had been killed, *sayyedina* 'Isa would then follow the way of *sayyedina* Muhammad, breaking all the crosses – because he is not the 'son' of God and he was not crucified – and marrying and having children and governing as a just ruler in accordance with the Qur'an and the Sunnah, and finally, after his death, being buried next to the Prophet Muhammad in Madina, where they will remain until they are brought back to life on the Day of Rising and Judgement, may the blessings and peace of Allah be on both of them:

> It has been related by Abu Hurayra, may Allah be pleased with him, that the Prophet Muhammad, may Allah bless him and grant him peace, said, 'By the One in Whose hand my soul is, the son of Maryam will soon descend among you as a just judge, and he will break the crosses, and kill pigs, and abolish the *jizya,* and wealth will pour forth to such an extent that no one will accept it, and one *sajda* will be better than the world and what it contains.' Then Abu Hurayra added, 'If you wish, you can recite, **'And there is not one of the People of the Book but will certainly believe in him before his death – and on the Day of Standing he will be a witness against them.' (4.159)**. (Al-Bukhari).

And:

> It has been related by Abu Hurayra, may Allah be pleased with him, that the Prophet Muhammad, may Allah bless him and grant him peace, said, 'The Prophets are like brothers: they have different mothers but their *deen* is one. I am the closest of all the people to Jesus son of Mary, because there is no other Prophet between him and myself. He will come again, and when you see him, you will recognise him. He is of medium height and his colouring is reddish-white. He will be wearing two garments, and his hair will look wet. He will break the cross, kill the pigs, abolish the *jizya* and call the people to Islam. During his time, Allah will end every religion and sect other than Islam, and will destroy the Dajjal. Then peace and security will prevail on earth, so that lions will graze with camels, tigers with cattle, and wolves with sheep; children will be able to play with snakes without coming to any harm. Jesus will remain for forty years, then die, and the Muslims will pray for him.' (Ahmad ibn Hanbal: Musnad, 2.406).

And:

It has been related by Abu Hurayra, may Allah be pleased with him, that the Prophet Muhammad, may Allah bless him and grant him peace, said, 'What will you do when the son of Maryam descends amongst you and leads you as one of you?' Ibn Abi Dhi'b, on the authority of Abu Hurayra narrated 'your leader amongst you'. Ibn Abi Dhi'b said, 'Do you know what the words 'and leads you as one of you' mean?' I said, 'Explain these to me.' He said, 'He will lead you in accordance with the Book of your Lord, may He be glorified and exalted, and the Sunnah of your Messenger, may Allah bless him and grant him peace.' (Muslim).

And:

'Abd'Allah bin Amr reported sayyedina Muhammad, peace and blessings of Allah be upon him, as saying, 'Jesus, son of Mary, will descend to the earth, will marry, have children, and remain forty-five years, after which he will die and be buried along with me in my grave. Then Jesus, son of Mary, and I shall arise from one grave between Abu Bakr and 'Umar.' (Ibn al-Jauzi in *Kitab al-Wafa'*).

And:

It has been transmitted by 'Abdullah ibn 'Umar that the Prophet Muhammad, may Allah bless him and grant him peace, said, 'I dreamt at night that I was at the Ka'ba, and I saw a dark man like the most handsome of dark men you have ever seen. He had hair reaching to between his ears and his shoulders like the most excellent of such hair that you have seen. He had combed his hair, and water was dripping from it. He was leaning on two men or on the shoulders of two men doing *tawaf* around Ka'ba. I asked, "Who is this?" It was said, "Al-Masih ibn Maryam." Then we were with a man with wiry hair and blind in his right eye, as if it was a floating grape. I asked, "Who is this?" It was said to me, "This is al-Masih ad-Dajjal."' (*Al-Muwatta'* of *Imam* Malik: 49.2.2).

Just as *sayyedina* Musa foretold the coming of both *sayyedina* 'Isa and *sayyedina* Muhammad, so *sayyedina* 'Isa foretold the coming of *sayyedina* Muhammad (who, as we have just seen, himself foretold the second coming of *sayyedina* 'Isa), may the blessings and peace of Allah be on all three of them and on their families and companions and sincere followers:

**And (remember) when 'Isa son of Maryam said, 'O Tribe of Israel, surely I am the Messenger of Allah to you, confirming what was (revealed) before me in the Torah, and bringing good news of a Messenger who will come after me, whose name is the Praised One (Ahmad).'**

('Ahmad' is one of the names of the Prophet Muhammad, may Allah bless him and grant him peace, meaning 'the Most Praiseworthy', 'the One who Distinguishes between Truth and Falsehood', and 'the Comforter'. Its equivalent in Greek is '*Parakletos*' or '*Parakleitos*', meaning 'the Comforter' or 'the Praised One'.)

**Yet when he came to them with clear proofs, they said, 'This is clearly magic.'**

**And who does greater wrong than the one who makes up a lie against Allah when he is called to Islam? And Allah does not guide people who do wrong.**

**They desire to put out the Light of Allah with their words, but Allah will perfect His Light however much those who reject detest it.**

**He it is Who has sent His Messenger with the guidance and the true *deen*, so that He may make it overcome all other religions, however much the idol-worshippers detest it.**

**O you who trust, shall I lead you to a bargain that will save you from a painful punishment? You should believe in Allah and His Messenger, and fight in the way of Allah with your wealth and your selves. That is better for you, if only you knew.**

**He will forgive you your wrong actions and bring you into Gardens underneath which rivers flow, and pleasant dwellings in Gardens of Eden. That is the supreme success.**

**And He will give you something else that you love: Help from Allah and victory that is near – and give good news to the believers!** (61.6-13).

And:

**Allah is the Light of the heavens and the earth. The likeness of His light is as if there were a niche and in the niche is a lamp and in the lamp is a glass and the glass as it were a brilliant star, lit from a blessed tree, an olive, neither of the east nor of the west, whose oil is well nigh luminous, though fire has scarce touched it, Light upon Light. Allah guides the ones He wants to His light, and Allah strikes metaphors for mankind, and Allah knows all things. (Qur'an: 24.35)**

The last Messenger to be sent by Allah, not only to the Tribe of Israel, but to all mankind, and the *jinn*, was the Prophet Muhammad, may Allah bless him and grant him peace:

**And Allah indeed made a covenant with the Tribe of Israel, and We raised up twelve leaders from among them, and Allah said: 'Surely I am with you. If you establish the prayer and pay the *zakat*, and accept My Messengers and honour them, and lend to Allah a good loan, surely I will remit your sins, and surely I will bring you into Gardens underneath which rivers flow. So whoever of you disbelieves after this will certainly go astray from the right way.'**

**And because of their breaking their covenant, We have cursed them and made their hearts grow hard. They separate words from their meanings and forget about part of what they have been reminded; and you will not cease finding treachery from all except a few of them – but forgive them and pardon them. Surely Allah loves those who do good.**

> **And We made a covenant with those who say, 'Surely we are Christians,' but they forgot a part of what they had been reminded – so We have stirred up enmity and hatred among them until the Day of Standing, when Allah will show them what they were doing.**
>
> **O People of the Book, now has Our Messenger (Muhammad) indeed come to you, making clear to you much of what you used to hide in the Book, and forgiving much.**
>
> **Now there has indeed come to you from Allah a Light and a clear Book, whereby Allah guides whoever seeks His pleasure to paths of peace – and He brings them out of darkness into light by His decree, and guides them to a straight path.** (5.12-16).

As the above passage indicates, it was inevitable that when the Prophet Muhammad, may Allah bless him and grant him peace, began to call people to only worship Allah, many of them would be those who claimed to be following either *sayyedina* Musa or *sayyedina* 'Isa, and it is for this reason that there are so many *ayat* in the Qur'an which are addressed to such people.

As we have already seen earlier in this chapter, the Jewish priesthood did not succeed in having *sayyedina* 'Isa killed, even though they tried.

It was as a direct result of their rejecting *sayyedina* Zakariyya and *sayyedina* Yahya and *sayyedina* 'Isa, peace be on them, and because of their repeated and unsuccessful attempts to throw off the yoke of Roman domination, that the Temple of *sayyedina* Sulayman was destroyed for the second time, this time by the Romans, in 70 CE, and all Jews were banished from in and around Jerusalem and forced to disperse and wander elsewhere.

It was certainly at this point, if not before, that the Ark appears to have disappeared entirely, and if anyone other than Allah knows where it is today, then they are keeping it a closely guarded secret.

During the centuries that followed, the distinction between the Jews who had rejected *sayyedina* 'Isa and the Jews who had accepted him became more marked. Indeed 'the Jews' were now identified as those who claimed to be following *sayyedina* Musa but not *sayyedina* 'Isa – whereas those who claimed to be following *both sayyedina* Musa and *sayyedina* 'Isa – since there was no contradiction between their respective teachings – initially became known as 'the Nazarenes', and then eventually as 'the Christians', a term which although initially used to describe the Unitarian followers of *sayyedina* 'Isa was subsequently applied to anyone who claimed to be following *sayyedina* 'Isa, irrespective of whether or not they were Unitarian or Trinitarian or Roman Catholic or Greek Orthodox or any other variety.

Thus it was at a later stage, and once the Paulinian Trinitarian version of Christianity had eventually become enshrined as the official Roman and Greek religion, that 'the Christians' became identified simply as those who claimed to be following *sayyedina* 'Isa, peace be on him. Although they acknowledged that *sayyedina* Musa, peace be on him, had been a Prophet of God, they now claimed – thanks to Paul's experience on the road to Damascus, and in spite of it being recorded that *sayyedina* 'Isa had said that he had come to uphold the *shari'a* of *sayyedina* Musa and not to change it by even one jot or tittle – that they now had a 'new' covenant with God – which, in practical terms, enabled them to avoid following the *shari'a* of *sayyedina* Musa and *sayyedina* 'Isa, peace be on them, whenever it suited them.

Furthermore, by elevating *sayyedina* 'Isa to godhood, the Christians ensured that this logically meant that he must be far greater than any human Messenger before him, while the logic of the twin doctrines of the new covenant and of the atonement and forgiveness of sins – which, as we have already seen were originally invented by Paul of Tarsus, and then subsequently developed and fortified by St Augustine's doctrine of original sin in the 5th century CE – demanded that there was no need for any messenger after *sayyedina* 'Isa, which in turn implied that therefore anyone who claimed to be a Messenger after *sayyedina* 'Isa, peace be on him, must be a false prophet.

It was for these reasons that the Trinitarian Christians have consistently waged war on the Muslims – in sharp contrast to the Unitarian Christians who were far more able to recognise, understand and accept the simplicity and truth of the teachings of the Prophet Muhammad, may Allah bless him and grant him peace.

Thus during the first six centuries after the departure of *sayyedina* 'Isa, two very different religions were developed – Talmudic Judaism by 'the Jews' who devoted much of their energy to justifying their rejection of *sayyedina* 'Isa by means of their painstaking 'reinterpretation' of the Taurah, in the Talmud – and Christianity by 'the Christians' who, as we have already seen, split into two main groups, the Unitarians and the Trinitarians.

With the coming of *sayyedina* Muhammad, may Allah bless him and grant him peace, the definition of what it was to be a 'Jew' or a 'Christian' was further developed, in that 'the Jews' were now identified as those who claimed to be following *sayyedina* Musa but not *sayyedina* 'Isa and not *sayyedina* Muhammad, while 'the Christians' were now identified as those who claimed to be following *sayyedina* 'Isa but not *sayyedina* Musa and not *sayyedina* Muhammad, may the blessings and peace of Allah be on them.

As the definitions of what it was to be a 'Jew' and what it was to be a 'Christian' gradually and almost imperceptibly shifted and changed, the original connection which had existed between the followers of *sayyedina* Musa and the followers of *sayyedina* 'Isa with the twelve tribes of the Tribe of Israel was weakened to such an extent that in the end this connection came to be regarded as almost entirely irrelevant, especially in Europe, where the *shari'a* of *sayyedina* Musa and *sayyedina* 'Isa was in many respects largely abandoned, with only certain aspects of the teachings of these two great Prophets being absorbed into the European versions of the religions of Judaism and Christianity which had slowly developed into their own particular forms during the passage of time. Whereas both *sayyedina* Musa and *sayyedina* 'Isa had been sent specifically to the Tribe of Israel – their teachings were not intended for those who did not belong to the Tribe of Israel – an increasing number of 'Jews' and 'Christians' now belonged to different tribes and different races whose only connection with the Tribe of Israel was that they were all descended from *sayyedina* Nuh and *sayyedina* Adam – along with the rest of mankind – if you were only able to trace their genealogy back far enough.

Thus European Judaism and European Christianity soon became very different to Middle Eastern and North African Judaism and Christianity, not only in terms of linguistic content and understanding, but also in terms of formal behaviour and life patterning, even though they were all derived from a common source.

The most notable example of a people who did not belong to the Tribe of Israel embracing Judaism is that of the Khazars, a turkic tribe who lived in the area of land that lies between the Black sea and the Caspian sea, the traditional homeland of Gog and Magog. This tribe embraced Judaism in the 8th century CE, for reasons of political expediency, and its descendants – who are today known either as 'the thirteenth tribe' or more commonly as the Ashkenazi Jews – subsequently spread up into Russia, across into the rest of Europe, over to America, and then all over the world, including the Holy Land.

Today the Ashkenazi Jews far outnumber the Sephardhic or Oriental Jews, who still have some genealogical link, however tenuous, with the tribes of Levi and Judah and part of the tribe of Benjamin – who, it will be remembered, were the two and a half of the twelve tribes of the Tribe of Israel who had once comprised the southern kingdom of Judah after the former kingdom of *sayyedina* Sulayman had split in two after his death.

Whereas the followers of Judaism have tended, although widely scattered, to remain relatively limited in number, the followers of Christianity have become far more numerous. This is because the followers of Judaism consider themselves a 'chosen' people, a 'race' apart, and accordingly they do not usually try to convert anyone else to Judaism – whereas the followers of Christianity believe that only those who are Christians will be 'saved' and accordingly they try and 'save' as many people as possible by converting them to Christianity. Thus today virtually every race in the world has a 'Christian' element.

Given this philosophy and its consequences, very few Christians can truthfully claim to be descended from the original Tribe of Israel, with the exception perhaps of some Middle Eastern and North African Christians who may be descended from the nine and a half tribes of the Tribe of Israel who, it will be remembered, once comprised the northern kingdom of Israel after the former kingdom of *sayyedina* Sulayman had split in two, and who, it is usually alleged by Jewish historians, mysteriously disappeared from history after the Assyrian invasion in approximately 722 BC.

As we have already seen in Chapter Seven, the most likely explanation for this 'disappearance' is that many of the descendants of the nine and a half tribes of the northern kingdom of Israel most probably became Christians after the coming of *sayyedina* 'Isa, and then Muslims after the coming of *sayyedina* Muhammad, may the blessings and peace of Allah be on them.

Since there are so many *ayat* in the Qur'an which are addressed to 'the Jews' and 'the Christians' – whether they are descended from the Tribe of Israel or not, and today there are not many who can make such a claim – it would be helpful to consider at least some of these *ayat*.

Although many of these *ayat* may appear to have been directed primarily towards the followers of Middle Eastern and North African Judaism and Christianity who were alive when the Qur'an was first revealed during the 7th century CE, it is clear that they often apply equally, if not more so, to the followers of the various European versions of Judaism and Christianity which, as we have already seen, developed at a later stage – and it is equally clear that they still often apply towards today's Jews and Christians, whatever version of Judaism or Christianity they may now claim to be following.

# Chapter Eleven

# The People of the Book

By the time of the coming of *sayyedina* Muhammad, may Allah bless him and grant him peace, the group of people who claimed to be the guardians and followers of the teachings of *sayyedina* Musa had become known as 'the Jews'. They claimed that *sayyedina* 'Isa was not the long awaited Messiah (for whom they still claim to be waiting today), that *sayyedina* Muhammad was not a Messenger of Allah, and that only they were rightly guided.

Similarly, the group of people who claimed still to be the guardians and followers of the teachings of *sayyedina* 'Isa had become known as 'the Christians'. They accepted that *sayyedina* Musa had been a Messenger of Allah, but claimed that *sayyedina* 'Isa had brought a new covenant, that *sayyedina* Muhammad was not a Messenger of Allah, and that only they would be saved on the Day of Resurrection.

It should be remembered that both *sayyedina* Musa and *sayyedina* 'Isa, peace be on them, were sent specifically to the Tribe of Israel, and that during the period in which the Qur'an was revealed the majority of the people in the Middle East and North Africa who described themselves either as Jews or as Christians were still descendants of the twelve tribes of the Tribe of Israel – although as we have just seen, the European versions of Judaism and Christianity were, by then, beginning to take a firmer hold among people who did not belong to the Tribe of Israel.

It was only during the centuries following the Prophet Muhammad's death in 11 AH/632 CE, may Allah bless him and grant him peace, that the religions of Judaism and Christianity were seriously adopted and adapted and further redefined by people for whom the Taurah and the Ingil were never intended – that is, by people who were not descended from the Tribe of Israel.

There are many *ayat* in the Qur'an addressed either to the Jews, or to the Christians, or to both groups together, in which they are described either as Jews and Christians or as 'the Tribe of Israel' or as 'the People of the Book', a title indicating – more then than now – both their common genealogical link with the Tribe of Israel as well as the fact that their way of life was at least to some extent still based on one of the earlier divine revelations.

It would be instructive to consider some of these *ayat*, since they not only clarify what the original nature and content of the teachings of *sayyedina* Musa and *sayyedina* 'Isa were – and this includes the teachings of all the Prophets and Messengers who were sent during the period between them – but also confirm how these teachings were changed at a later stage by those who claimed still to be following them.

Accordingly we will first consider those *ayat* which are addressed principally to the Jews, then those which are addressed principally to the Christians, and finally those which are addressed in more general terms to either one or both of these groups as 'the People of the Book'.

## THE JEWS

In describing the Jews Allah says:

> **Have you any hope that they will be true to you – when a party of them used to listen to the Word of Allah, then used to change it, after they had understood it, intentionally?**
>
> **And when they meet those who believe, they say, 'We believe' – but when they meet each other in private, they say, 'Are you going to tell them what Allah has revealed to you so that they will argue about it with you before your Lord?'**
>
> **Do you not understand?**

Do they not realise that Allah knows what they conceal and what they make public?

And among them are those who are illiterate, who do not know the Book except as they imagine it, and so they are only guessing.

So woe to those who write the Book with their own hands and then say, 'This is from Allah', so that they can make some gain with it. Woe to them for what their hands have written, and woe to them for what they earn from it.

And they say, 'The Fire will not touch us, except for a certain number of days.'

Say: 'Have you received a covenant from Allah? – for Allah never breaks His promise – or are you saying what you do not know about Allah?'

Indeed – and whoever has done evil and is surrounded by his sins, these are the companions of the Fire – there they will dwell for ever.

And those who trust and have good actions, these are the companions of the Garden – there they will dwell for ever.

And (remember) when We made a covenant with the Tribe of Israel (saying), 'Do not worship (anything) except Allah and be good to parents, and to relatives, and to orphans, and to the poor; and speak good to people; and establish the prayer; and pay the *zakat;*' – and then all but a few of you turned away in aversion.

And (remember) when We made a covenant with you (saying), 'Do not shed your own blood, and do not drive each other out from your homes,' and then you confirmed it and you were witnesses (to it).

And then in spite of this, you kill each other and drive out a group of yourselves from their homes, assisting each other

**against them with wickedness and enmity – and if they came to you as captives, then you would ransom them, even though it was unlawful for you to have driven them out (in the first place).**

**Do you accept part of the Book and reject part of it?**

**And what is the reward for those of you who do that except shame in the life of this world – and on the Day of Standing they will be driven towards the most intense punishment – and Allah will not forget about what you were doing.**

**These are the ones who buy the life of this world at the expense of the next world – and the punishment will not be lightened for them, and they will not be helped.**

**And We indeed gave Musa the Book, and We made a succession of Messengers follow after him, and We gave 'Isa ibn Maryam clear proofs and We helped him with the holy spirit (Jibril).**

**So why is it that whenever a Messenger comes to you with what you yourselves do not want, you become arrogant, rejecting some, and killing some?**

**And they say, 'Our hearts are covered over.'**

**Indeed Allah has cursed them for their disbelief – and what they do believe is very little.**

**And when a Book from Allah comes to them, confirming what they already have – and before this they were asking for a clear explanation regarding those who reject – when there comes to them what they recognise (to be true), they reject it; and so the curse of Allah is on those who reject.**

**The price for which they have sold their selves is a miserable one – rejecting what Allah has revealed, and begrudging that out of His generosity Allah has given a revelation for whomever of His slaves that He wishes; and so they**

**have incurred anger upon anger – and for those who reject there is a shameful punishment.**

**And when it is said to them, 'Believe in what Allah has revealed,' they say, 'We believe in what has been revealed to us,' and they reject what has come after it, even though it is the truth confirming what they already have.**

**Say: 'So why did you kill Prophets of Allah in the past, if you (really) are believers?'**

**And Musa certainly came to you with clear proofs, but you chose the calf in his absence, and you were wrong doers.**

**And (remember) when We made a covenant with you, and made Mount Tur tower over you, (saying), 'Hold fast to what We have given you and listen!' they said, 'We hear and we disobey!' – and (love of) the calf sank into their hearts because of their disbelief.**

**Say: 'What your belief demands of you is despicable, if you are (really) believers.'**

**Say: 'If the abode of the next world with Allah is exclusively for you, and not for the rest of mankind, then long for death if you are speaking the truth.'**

**But they will never long for it, because of what their actions have sent ahead of them – and Allah knows all about the wrong doers.**

**And you will find them the greediest of mankind for this life, even more than those who worship idols: each of them would love to live for a thousand years – and even to live that long would not make him escape the punishment – and Allah sees what they do. (2.75-96).**

It is interesting, as regards these last *ayat*, to consider the following passage from *Ash-Shifa'* of *Qadi* 'Iyad, taken from the section which considers the inimitability of the Qur'an:

Another clear facet of its inimitability are the *ayat* related about people's incapacity in certain cases to respond to a particular challenge whilst informing them that they would not meet it. Then they were indeed unable to do so. This is illustrated by what Allah says to the Jews: **'Say: "If you have the Abode of the Next World exclusively ... then long for death if you are speaking the truth."'** (2.94).

Abu Ishaq az-Zajjaj said, "This *ayah* provides the greatest proof and clearest indication of the soundness of His Message because He told them, 'Long for death,' and informed the Jews that they would never long for it and subsequently none of them longed for it. The Prophet said, 'By the One in whose hand my soul is, not a man of them could say that without choking on his spit,' i.e. dying where he stood. (Al-Bayhaqi). So Allah turned the Jews away from longing for death and terrified them in order to manifest the truthfulness of His Messenger and the soundness of what had been revealed to him since none of them really wished for death although they would have been eager to reject him if they had been able to do so. But Allah does what He wills. By this *ayah* his miracles were evident and his proof was clear."

Abu Muhammad al-Usayli said, "An amazing thing about this business is that there was not a single group or individual among the Jews from the day that Allah commanded His Prophet to say this who came forward against him or answered him. It remained available as a pretext for anyone among them who wanted to put him to the test." (*Ash-Shifa'* of *Qadi* 'Iyad: 1.4.8).

There is also a similar passage in Surat al-Jumu'a:

**The metaphor of those who are entrusted with the Taurah and then do not apply it is like the donkey carrying books – what a miserable likeness for the people who deny the signs of Allah – and Allah does not guide the people who do wrong.**

**Say: 'O you who are Jews, if you claim that you are the friends of Allah, and not the rest of mankind, then long for death if you are being truthful.'**

**And they will never long for it, because of the (deeds) their hands have sent on ahead of them – and Allah knows who are the wrongdoers.**

**Say: 'Surely the death from which you flee will surely meet you. Then you will be returned to the Knower of the Unseenand the Seen, and He will tell you about what you used to do. (62.5-8).**

Another reference to the Jews' killing some of the Prophets who were sent to them after the time of *sayyedina* Musa is to be found in Surat al-Ma'idah:

**We indeed made a covenant with the Tribe of Israel, and We sent Messengers to them. Whenever a Messenger came to them with anything which their selves did not want, some they denied and some they killed.**

**And they supposed that there would be no test, so they became blind and deaf, and then Allah relented towards them, and then afterwards many of them again became blind and deaf – and Allah sees what they do. (5.70-71).**

It was because of their becoming blind and deaf to the signs of Allah that the Tribe of Israel were eventually invaded twice:

**And We gave Musa the Book, and We made it a guidance for the Tribe of Israel, (saying), 'Do not choose any guardian other than me!'**

**They were the descendants of those whom We carried (in the ship) with Nuh – surely he was a grateful slave.**

**And We decreed for the Tribe of Israel in the Book: 'You will certainly spread corruption in the earth twice, and you will certainly become great tyrants.'**

**And so when the first of the two warnings came to pass, We sent slaves of Ours who were extremely powerful against**

**you, and they plundered your dwellings completely – and it was a warning which was fulfilled.**

**Then We restored mastery over them back to you, and We increased your wealth and children, and We made your numbers more, (saying), 'If you do good, you do yourselves good – and if you do evil, then that is what you have.'**

**And when the second of the two warnings came to pass, (We sent more slaves of Ours) to bring despair to your faces, and to enter the Temple just as they entered it the first time, and to utterly destroy whatever was in their power.**

**It may be that your Lord will have mercy on you – but if you turn away (from Us), We will turn away (from you) – and We have made Hell a prison for those who reject.** (17.2-8).

It is generally agreed by the commentators on the Qur'an that the 'first' destruction referred to in the above passage was the invasion of King Nebuchadnezzar in 586 BC, when the Temple of Sulayman was destroyed, and many of the Tribe of Israel were taken back to Babylon as slaves.

And it is generally agreed by the commentators on the Qur'an that the 'second' destruction referred to in the above passage was the occupation of Palestine by the Romans which coincided with the coming of *sayyedina* 'Isa, peace be on him, and which culminated in the destruction, for the second time, of the Temple of Sulayman in 70 CE, after which it has never been rebuilt.

It was largely as a result of these two major events that the 'Tribe of Israel' became scattered and dispersed, initially throughout the Middle East and North Africa, and subsequently throughout the world – although as we have already seen at the end of Chapter Four, it was in fact as a result of the Assyrian invasion in 722 BC that nine and a half of the twelve tribes of the Tribe of Israel appear to have already abruptly and mysteriously 'disappeared' from the annals of Jewish history and are never subsequently referred to again by Jewish historians either as belonging to the Tribe of Israel or as Jews.

As we have already seen, it was the remaining two tribes – the tribes of Judah and Levi, (together with some of the tribe of Benjamin) – who appointed themselves the guardians of the teachings of *sayyedina* Musa, peace be on him, and who subsequently became known as 'the Jews', a title which most probably derives from the abbreviated form of either Judah or Judea. It was this relatively small remnant of the original Tribe of Israel who subsequently rewrote the Taurah more than once, and who – after rejecting *sayyedina* 'Isa, peace be on him – further redefined its contents by means of written commentary and reinterpretation more than once, and from whom the Sephardhic and Oriental Jews are largely descended.

It should also be emphasised in passing that the turkic Tribe of the Khazars – who, as we have already seen, were originally settled in the Caucasus between the Black sea and the Caspian sea, and who embraced Judaism for reasons of political expediency during the 8th century CE, and from whom the Ashkenazi Jews are largely descended – are *not* descended from any of the twelve tribes of the Tribe of Israel, with whom they have no linguistic or genealogical connection, other than the fact that they are all ultimately descended from *sayyedina* Adam and *sayyedina* Nuh – along with the rest of mankind – the Sephardhic or Oriental Jews being descended from Shem, the son of Nuh, and the Khazar or Ashkenazi Jews being descended from Yafeth, the son of Nuh – which is why they are sometimes described as 'the thirteenth tribe'!

As Allah points out in the Qur'an, part of the Jews' being blind and deaf to the signs of Allah manifests in their keeping what has been revealed to them concealed – not only from other people but even from their own people:

> **And they do not measure the power of Allah truthfully when they say, 'Allah has not revealed anything to a human being.'**
>
> **Say: 'Who revealed the Book which Musa brought – a light and a guidance for mankind – which you have put on scrolls which you display while hiding much of it, and (from**

**which) you have learned what neither you nor your fathers knew about?'**

**Say: 'Allah!' and then leave them to their useless talk! (6.91).**

It is also clear from the Qur'an that part of what the Jews have done is not only to conceal parts of what was revealed to them in the Taurah, but also to actually change its contents. And whoever changes the revelations of Allah is asking for trouble:

**Ask the Tribe of Israel how many clear signs We gave them – and as for whoever changes the blessing of Allah after it has come to him, then surely Allah is severe in punishment. (2.211).**

Allah also says:

**And who is more in the wrong than someone who makes up something about Allah which is a lie, or who says, 'I am inspired!' when he is not inspired at all, and who says, 'I will reveal the like of what Allah has revealed!'?**

**If you could see when the wrong doers are in the agonies of death, and the angels stretch out their hands (saying), 'Give up your selves! Today you will be rewarded with a shameful punishment because of what you said about Allah which was not true, and because you treated His signs with scorn.' (6.93).**

And:

**Surely those who conceal anything of the Book which Allah has revealed, and purchase a small gain thereby, eat nothing but fire in their bellies; and Allah will not speak to them on the Day of Standing, He will not purify them, and for them there is a painful punishment. These are the ones who exchange error for guidance, and punishment for forgiveness. How determined they are on their way to the Fire!**

**That is because Allah has revealed the Book with the truth. And surely those who seek to disagree over what is in the Book are in deep schism. (2.174-177).**

And:

**As for those who hide the clear proofs and the guidance which We have revealed – after We have made it clear to mankind in the Book – surely they are accursed by Allah and accursed by those who have the power to curse, except for those who repent and make amends and make manifest (the truth) and these it is towards whom I relent – and I am the Relenting, the Compassionate.**

**As for those who reject, and who die in disbelief, surely on them is the curse of Allah and of the angels and of all mankind. (2.159-161).**

It is as a result of all the alterations – both in the original text and also by means of redefinitions achieved by means of 'interpretations' and 'commentaries' – to which the original teachings of *sayyedina* Musa have been subjected, that many of the Jews – who even to this day continue to reject *sayyedina* 'Isa and *sayyedina* Muhammad – have always argued amongst themselves, as Allah points out in the following *ayat*:

**And We indeed gave Musa the Book, and there has been disagreement about it – and if it had not been for a decree which had already come from your Lord, judgement concerning them would certainly have been passed – and surely they are hopelessly in doubt about it. (11.110 and 41.45).**

And:

**And We indeed gave the Tribe of Israel the Book and the Command and the Prophethood, and We provided them with good things and We favoured them the most in all the worlds. And We gave them clear commandments – and they did not disagree until after knowledge had come to them, out of rivalry amongst themselves. Surely your Lord will**

**judge between them on the Day of Standing concerning what they used to disagree about. (45.16-17).**

And:

**And they did not become divided until after knowledge had come to them, out of rivalry amongst themselves, and if it had not been for a decree for an appointed term which had already come from your Lord, judgement concerning them would certainly have been passed – and surely those who have inherited the Book after them are hopelessly in doubt about it. (42.14).**

And:

**And We indeed gave Musa the Book – so do not be in any doubt about his receiving it – and We made it a guidance for the Tribe of Israel, and when they became steadfast and were certain about Our signs, then We chose *imams* from among them who guided by Our command.**

**Surely your Lord will judge between them on the Day of Standing concerning what they used to disagree about. (32.23-25).**

And:

**Surely the sabbath was only decreed for those who disagreed about it – and surely your Lord will certainly judge between them on the Day of Standing concerning what they used to disagree about. (16.124).**

And:

**Surely this Qur'an explains most of what the Tribe of Israel disagree about, and it is most certainly a guidance and a mercy for the believers.**

**Surely your Lord will judge between them in His wisdom – and He is the Mighty, the Knowing. (27.76-78).**

The following passage from Surat an-Nisa is more specific:

**The People of the Book ask you to make a Book come down to them from the heaven – and they indeed asked Musa (to do) more than that when they said, 'Let us see Allah clearly,' so the lightning struck them for their wrong doing; and then they chose the calf after clear proofs had come to them – and We forgave them for that – and We gave Musa clear authority.**

**And We made Mount Tur tower over them when they made their covenant, and We said to them, 'Enter the gate prostrating!' and We said to them, 'Do not break the sabbath!' and We took a firm covenant from them.**

**And because of their breaking their covenant, and their rejecting the signs of Allah, and their killing the Prophets without any justification, and their saying, 'Our hearts are covered over,'– indeed Allah has set a seal on them because of their disbelief, so that they will not believe except for a few – and because of their disbelief and their spreading a great slander against Maryam, and their saying, 'Surely we killed the Messiah, 'Isa son of Maryam', a Messenger of Allah –**

**And they did not kill him and they did not crucify him, but it appeared so to them. And surely those who disagree about it are certainly in doubt about it – they have no knowledge about it except that they follow speculation.**

**And they did not kill him for certain – but Allah took him up to Himself. And Allah was ever Mighty, Wise.**

**And there is not one of the People of the Book but will certainly believe in him before his death – and on the Day of Standing he will be a witness against them.**

**– And because of the wrong doing of the Jews, We forbade them the good things which were permitted for them (before), and because of their turning away from the way of**

**Allah so much, and their taking usury – and they were indeed forbidden it – and their devouring people's wealth through deception, We have prepared a painful punishment for those of them who disbelieve.**

**But those of them who are firm in knowledge, and the believers, believe in what has been revealed to you (Muhammad), and in what has been revealed before you – and those who establish the prayer, and those who pay the *zakat*, and those who believe in Allah and the Last Day – to these we shall give a great reward. (4.153-162).**

It is ironic that although the Qur'an does clarify most of what the Tribe of Israel – and subsequently the Jews – came to disagree about, the majority of them in every age since the Qur'an was first revealed, have also chosen to disagree with what is in the Qur'an as well, especially since one of the facts of which it reminds them is that the original Taurah foretold the coming of not only *sayyedina* 'Isa, but also of *sayyedina* Muhammad, may Allah bless them both and grant them peace. Thus when describing those who believe in the signs of Allah – including the Prophet Muhammad, may Allah bless him and grant him peace – Allah says :

**Those who follow the Messenger, the Prophet who can neither read nor write, whom they will find described in the Taurah and the Ingil which are with them – he will enjoin what is right on them and forbid them what is wrong, and he will make the good things lawful for them and prohibit them the foul things, and he will relieve them of their burden and the chains they used to wear.**

**So those who believe in him, and honour him, and help him, and follow the light which is sent down with him – they are the successful ones. (7.157).**

And, referring to the revelation of the Qur'an – and therefore to the coming of Muhammad, may Allah bless him and grant him peace:

**And surely it is certainly in the earlier scriptures – is it not a sign for them that the people of knowledge of the Tribe of Israel know about it? (26.196-197).**

The following passage from *Ash-Shifa'* of *Qadi* 'Iyad is also of interest in this context:

'Ata ibn Yasar said, "I met 'Abdullah ibn 'Amr ibn al-'As and said, 'Describe the Messenger of Allah to me.' He replied, 'Certainly! By Allah, some of the characteristics by which he is described in the Qur'an can also be found in the Torah. It says: "O Prophet, We have sent you as a witness, a bringer of good news and a warner and a refuge for the unlettered. You are My slave and My Messenger. I have called you the one on whom people rely, one who is neither coarse nor vulgar and who neither shouts in the markets nor repays evil with evil, but rather pardons and forgives. Allah will not take him back to Himself until the crooked community has been straightened out by him and they say, 'There is no god but Allah.' Through him, blind eyes, deaf ears and covered hearts will be opened.'" Something similar is reported from Abdullah ibn Salam and Ka'b al-Ahbar.

One path of transmission from Ibn Ishaq has, "Who does not shout in the markets nor use obscene language nor indecent words. I open him to every excellent quality and I give him every noble trait. I make tranquillity his garment, devotion his motto, fear of Allah his conscience, wisdom his understanding, truthfulness and loyalty his nature, pardon and correct behaviour his character, justice his behaviour, the truth his *shari'a,* guidance his leader, Islam his religion and Ahmad his name. I will guide him after misguidance and I will teach him after ignorance. I will elevate him after obscurity. I will make his name known after non-recognition. I will give him much after scarcity. I will enrich him after poverty. I will gather him after separation. I will bring together separated hearts and scattered passions and separate communities through him. I will make his community the best community that has come forth to people."

> In another hadith, the Messenger of Allah told us about the way he was described in the Torah: "My slave, Ahmad, the Chosen, born in Makka, who will emigrate to Madina (or he said Tayyiba), his community will be those who praise Allah in every state." (Related by ad-Darimi from Ka'b; and by at-Tabarani and Abu Nu'aym from Ibn Mas'ud). (*Ash-Shifa* of *Qadi* 'Iyad: I.1.2).

Many of the Jews who lived during the time of the Prophet Muhammad, may Allah bless him and grant him peace, recognised who he was from the descriptions of him in the Torah. Only a few of them embraced Islam as a result, while many of them remained determined to oppose him.

Safiyya bint Huyayy, for example, who was one of the wives of the Prophet Muhammad, may the blessings and peace of Allah be on him and his family and companions, and who was descended from *sayyedina* Harun, the brother of *sayyedina* Musa, was a member of the Jewish tribe of the Banu Nadir. When talking about her childhood, it has been related that she said:

> I was my father's favourite and also a favourite with my uncle Abu Yasir. They could never see me with one of their children without picking me up. When the Messenger of Allah, may Allah bless him and grant him peace, came to Madina, my father and uncle went to see him. It was very early in the morning, between dawn and sunrise. They did not return until the sun was setting. They came back worn out and depressed, walking with slow, heavy steps. I smiled to them as I always did, but neither of them took any notice of me because they were so miserable. I heard Abu Yasir ask my father:
>
> 'Is it him?'
>
> 'Yes, it is.'
>
> 'Can you recognise him? Can you verify it?'
>
> 'Yes, I can recognise him only too well.'
>
> 'What do you feel towards him?'
>
> 'Enmity, enmity as long as I live.' (*The Wives of the Prophet* by Ahmad Thomson, pp.68-69, referring to *As-Sirat ar-Rasulu'llah* by Muhammad Ibn Ishaq, pp.354-355).

Another notable conversion to Islam by a Jew in the time of the Prophet Muhammad, may Allah bless him and grant him peace, was that of 'Abdullah ibn Salam of the Banu Qainuqa', one of the chief rabbis of the Jews. It has been transmitted by Anas that when he heard of the arrival of the Prophet Muhammad in Madina, 'Abdullah ibn Salam came to him and said, 'I will ask you three things about which only a Prophet would know: What is the first sign of the Hour (the end of the world)? What will be the first meal that the people of the Garden will eat? And why does a child resemble its father and why does it resemble its maternal uncle?'

The Prophet Muhammad, may Allah bless him and grant him peace, replied, 'Jibril has just told me the answers: As for the first sign of the Hour, it will be a fire that will bring together the people from the east to the west; and as for the first meal that the people of the Garden will eat, it will include fish liver; and as for the resemblance of a child – if a man has intercourse with his wife and his fluid comes before hers, then it will be like him – and if her fluid comes before his, then it will be like her.'

'Abdullah ibn Salam immediately said, 'I bear witness that you are the Messenger of Allah,' and then he added, 'O Messenger of Allah, the Jews are liars, and if they hear about my Islam before you ask them about me, they will tell you lies about me.' So when the Jews were coming, 'Abdullah went into the house, and the Messenger of Allah, may Allah bless him and grant him peace, said to them, 'What kind of a man is 'Abdullah ibn Salam amongst you?' They replied, 'He is the most learned person of us and the son of the most learned person of us, and the best of us and the son of the best of us.'

Then the Messenger of Allah, may Allah bless him and grant him peace, said, 'What would you think if 'Abdullah embraced Islam?' They replied. 'May Allah save him from that!' Then 'Abdullah came out to them and said, 'I bear witness that there is no god except Allah – and that Muhammad is the Messenger of Allah,' at which they said, 'He is the worst of us and the son of the worst of us!' and continued to slander him. (Al-Bukhari).

Thus it is clear from fully authenticated contemporary historical accounts that the Tribe of Israel, and subsequently the Jews, were always aware of the coming of the Prophet Muhammad, may Allah bless him and grant him peace, and accordingly Allah's invitation to the Jews has remained what it has always been:

> **O Tribe of Israel, remember My blessing with which I blessed you, and fulfil your covenant with Me – I will fulfil my covenant with you – and as for Me, fear Me!**
>
> **And believe in what I reveal, confirming what you already have, and do not be the first to reject it, and do not exchange My signs for something of little value – and as for Me, fear Me!**
>
> **And do not cover up the truth with falsehood or knowingly conceal the truth.**
>
> **And establish the prayer, and pay the *zakat*, and bow down in worship with those who bow down in worship.**
>
> **Would you call people to good action while you yourselves neglect it – and you recite the Book? Have you no intellect?**
>
> **And seek help in patience and the prayer, and surely that is very difficult except for those who are humble – those who know that they will surely meet their Lord and that surely they are returning to Him. (2.40-46).**

And:

> **O Tribe of Israel, remember My blessing with which I blessed you, and how I favoured you the most in all the worlds, and be aware of a Day when no self will be of any good to another self, and compensation will not be accepted from it, and intercession will not be of any use to it – and they will not be helped. (2.122-123).**

As for the Jews who refused to embrace Islam, the results of their actions remain what they have always been:

> **And Allah indeed made a covenant with the Tribe of Israel, and We raised up twelve leaders from among them, and Allah said: 'Surely I am with you. If you establish the prayer and pay the *zakat*, and accept My Messengers and honour them, and lend to Allah a good loan, surely I will remit your sins, and surely I will bring you into Gardens underneath which rivers flow. So whoever of you disbelieves after this will certainly go astray from the right way.'**
>
> **And because of their breaking their covenant, We have cursed them and made their hearts grow hard. They separate words from their meanings and forget about part of what they have been reminded; and you will not cease finding treachery from all except a few of them – but forgive them and pardon them. Surely Allah loves those who do good. (5.12-13).**

And:

> **Some of those who are Jews change the meanings of words and they say, 'We hear and we disobey', and, 'Hear without hearing and listen to us', twisting meaning with their tongues and insulting the *deen*.**
>
> **If only they had said, 'We hear and we obey', and, 'Hear and look at us', it would have been better for them and more proper; but Allah has cursed them for their rejecting, so they will not believe, except for a few. (4.46)**

The significance of the above *ayah* can only be understood if the reader is aware of the fact that the Jews used to intentionally mispronounce the Arabic word *'ra'ina'*, meaning 'listen to us' (which the Muslims used as a term of respect to attract the Prophet Muhammad's attention, may Allah bless him and grant him peace), so that it became an insult in the Hebrew language. It is for this reason that Allah tells the Muslims in Surat al-Baqara not to say *'ra'ina'*, but rather *'andhurna'*, meaning 'look at us', because this word does not take on another derogatory meaning in Hebrew if mispronounced:

> **O you who believe, do not say, 'Listen to us', but say, 'Look at us' – and listen – and there will be a painful punishment for those who reject. (2.104).**

Another of the favourite intentional mispronunciations of some of the Jews in the time of the Prophet Muhammad, may Allah bless him and grant him peace, was to greet both him and the Muslims by saying, *'as-samu alaikum'*, meaning 'death to you', (rather than using the Muslim greeting, *'as-salaamu alaikum'*, meaning 'peace on you'), which would be countered with, *'wa alaikum'*, meaning 'and the same to you!' (Muslim).

It was in connection with this practice of the Jews that the following *ayah* was revealed:

> **Have you not observed those who were forbidden to plot in secret – and how they have persisted in what they were forbidden, plotting evil and enmity and disobedience against the Messenger? – and when they come to you, they greet you with a greeting with which Allah does not greet you, and they say in themselves, 'Why should Allah punish us for what we say?' Hell will be enough for them – they will burn in it – what an awful journey's end! (58.8).**

It has also been related that the Jews used to try to sneeze in the presence of the Prophet Muhammad, may Allah bless him and grant him peace, hoping that he would say, 'May Allah have mercy on you!' – which is what he would say if a Muslim sneezed in his presence – but instead he would say, 'May Allah guide you and grant you well-being!' (Abu Da'ud).

Those Jews who mocked the Prophet Muhammad, may Allah bless him and grant him peace, and who refused to take him seriously were a source of sorrow for him, although Allah commanded him not to let their behaviour upset him:

> **O Messenger, do not let those who compete in disbelief grieve you, those who say 'We believe' with their mouths, but whose hearts do not believe, and those who are Jews,**

listeners for the sake of falsehood, listeners for other people who do not come to you themselves; they take words out of their context; they say, 'If you are given this, take it, but if this is not given to you, then beware!'

And as for whomever Allah wishes to test, you will not have any authority over him apart from Allah in the least. These are the ones whose hearts Allah does not wish to purify – for them there is disgrace in this world, and in the next world theirs will be a tremendous punishment.

Listeners for the sake of falsehood, devouring what is forbidden. So if they come to you, then judge between them, or decline their request. If you decline, then they cannot harm you at all, and if you give a judgement, then judge between them with equity – surely Allah loves those who are equitable.

And how can they come to you for judgement if they have the Taurah with them, in which is Allah's judgement? Yet even after that, they would turn away, for they are not from among the believers.

Surely We revealed the Taurah – in which there was guidance and light – by which the Prophets who submitted (to Allah) judged the Jews – and the rabbis and the priests, to whom the Book of Allah was entrusted for protection, and they were witnesses of it. So do not fear mankind, but fear Me; and do not exchange My signs for something of little value.

And whoever does not judge by what Allah has revealed, then they are people who reject.

And in it We prescribed for them the life for the life, and the eye for the eye, and the nose for the nose, and the ear for the ear, and the tooth for the tooth, and for wounds like for like – and for whoever dispensed with it as an act of charity, it would be an expiation for him.

**And whoever does not judge by what Allah has revealed, then they are wrong doers.**

**And We sent 'Isa son of Maryam in their footsteps, confirming what was before him in the Taurah; and We gave him the Ingil – in which there was guidance and light – confirming what was before it in the Taurah, and a guidance and a warning to those who have *taqwa.***

**And let the people of the Ingil judge by what Allah has revealed in it.**

**And whoever does not judge by what Allah has revealed, then they are evil livers.**

**And to you (O Muhammad) We have revealed the Book with truth, confirming the Book that was before it and preserving it. So judge between them by what Allah has revealed, and do not follow their desires, away from the truth that has come to you.**

**For every one of you We have appointed a divine law and an open way.**

**And if Allah had wanted, He could certainly have made you one community, but (things are as they are) so that He may test you through what He has given you. So compete with good actions. To Allah you will all return, and then He will tell you about whatever you used to disagree about.**

**So judge between them by what Allah has revealed, and do not follow their desires, and beware of them lest they lead you away from part of what Allah has revealed to you. And if they turn away, then know that surely Allah wishes to punish them for some wrong-action of theirs – and surely many of mankind are evil livers.**

**Are they looking for a judgement from the time of the *jahiliyya*? – And what is better than Allah's judgement for a people who are certain? (5.41-50).**

The above *ayat* were revealed after an incident in which some Jews came to the Prophet Muhammad, may Allah bless him and grant him peace, and asked him to judge two Jews who were both married and who had committed adultery with each other.

It has been transmitted by Abu Hurayra that the Prophet Muhammad, may Allah bless him and grant him peace, said to them, 'I ask you to swear by Allah Who revealed the Taurah to Musa, what do you find in the Taurah concerning a married person who commits adultery?' They replied, 'They are blackened with charcoal, and then taken around among the people back to back on a donkey, and then flogged.'

A young man who was with them remained silent, and when the Prophet Muhammad emphatically asked him to swear by Allah, he replied, 'By Allah, since you have asked us to swear, in the Taurah we find that they are to be stoned.'

When the Prophet Muhammad asked him when it was that the Jews had lightened the punishment, he replied, 'A relative of a certain king among our kings committed adultery, but he reprieved them from being stoned. Then a man of a family among the common people committed adultery, and he intended to have him stoned – but his people complained and said, "Our man should not be stoned until you bring your man and have him stoned." So they made a compromise between them on what the punishment should be.'

Then the Prophet Muhammad, may Allah bless him and grant him peace, said to them, 'I will decide in accordance with what the Taurah says,' and the two Jews were stoned to death. (Abu Da'ud).

The same or a similar incident is described in *Al-Muwatta'* of *Imam* Malik:

> Malik related to me from Nafi' that 'Abdullah ibn 'Umar said, 'The Jews came to the Messenger of Allah, may Allah bless him and grant him peace, and mentioned to him that a man and woman from among them had committed adultery.

'The Messenger of Allah, may Allah bless him and grant him peace, asked them, "What do you find in the Torah about stoning?" They said, "We make their wrong action known and flog them." 'Abdullah ibn Salam said, "You have lied! It has stoning for it, so bring the Torah." They spread it out and one of them placed his hand over the *ayat* of stoning. Then he read what was before it and what was after it. 'Abdullah ibn Salam told him to lift his hand. He lifted his hand and there was the *ayat* of stoning. They said, "He has spoken the truth, Muhammad. The *ayat* of stoning is in it." So the Messenger of Allah, may Allah bless him and grant him peace, gave the order and they were stoned.'

'Abdullah ibn 'Umar added, 'I saw the man leaning over the woman to protect her from the stones.' (*Al-Muwatta* of *Imam* Malik: 41.1.1).

The following *ayat* concerning giving judgement in accordance with what Allah has revealed are to be found in Surat al-An'am:

**Should I look for a judgement from other than Allah, when He is the One Who has revealed the Book, (the Qur'an) which explains (everything) clearly, to you?**

**And those to whom We gave the Book (in the past) know that it is certainly a true revelation from your Lord – so do not be among those who doubt. (6.114).**

The Qur'an also draws attention to some of the dietary laws of the Jews:

**All food was *halal* for the Tribe of Israel – except for what Israel (Ya'qub) made *haram* for himself – before the Taurah was revealed.**

**Say: 'Bring the Taurah and recite it, if you are truthful.'**

**And as for whoever makes up a lie about Allah after that – these are the wrong doers.**

**Say: 'Allah speaks the truth: so follow the way of Ibrahim, the *hanif*– and he was not one of those who worship idols.' (3.93-95).**

And:

**And We made every animal with claws *haram* for the Jews, and as for cattle and sheep, We made their fat *haram* for them, except for what is on their backs or entrails or what is mixed up with the bone – this is what We rewarded them with for their disobedience – and surely We are certainly speaking the truth.**

**So if they reject you, then say, 'The mercy of your Lord is all-embracing – but His punishment will not be withdrawn from sinful people.' (6.146-147).**

And:

**And we have made *haram* for the Jews what We have already told you of before – and We did not wrong them, but they used to wrong themselves. (16.118).**

It has been related that the Prophet Muhammad, may Allah bless him and grant him peace, once said, 'May Allah curse the Jews! They were forbidden to eat fat, so they sold it and ate its price.' (*Al-Muwatta* of *Imam* Malik: 49.10.26). In the Qur'an Allah severely reprimands the Jews for accusing Allah of what is in fact their own fault:

**And the Jews say, 'The hand of Allah is chained up.' It is their hands that are chained up – and they are cursed for what they say. Indeed His hands are spread out wide – he gives as He wishes.**

**And what has been revealed to you from your Lord is certain to increase the disobedience and disbelief of many of them; and We have placed enmity and hatred among them until the Day of Standing.**

**As often as they set fire to conflict, Allah puts it out; and they strive for corruption in the land – and Allah does not love those who are corrupt. (5.64).**

And:

**Allah has certainly heard the words of those who say, 'Surely Allah is poor, and we are rich.'**

**We shall record what they have said – and their killing the Prophets without any justification – and We shall say, 'Taste the burning punishment! This is what you prepared for yourselves – and surely Allah never wrongs His slaves.'**

**(These are) the ones who say, 'Surely Allah has commanded us not to believe in any Messenger until he brings us a sacrifice which is consumed by fire.'**

**Say (O Muhammad): 'Messengers have already come to you before me with clear signs – and with what you have just asked – so why did you kill them, if you can be truthful?'**

**And if they deny you, then they have already denied the Messengers before you, who came with clear signs, and with scriptures, and with the illuminating Book. (3.181-184).**

It has been transmitted by 'Abdullah ibn Mas'ud that the Prophet Muhammad, may Allah bless him and grant him peace, said, 'The first defect that permeated the Tribe of Israel was that one of them met another of them and said, "O so-and-so, have *taqwa* of Allah and leave what you are doing, because it is not *halal* for you." Then he met him again the next day and did not refuse to eat with him, and drink with him and sit with him – and when they did this, Allah mingled their hearts with each other.' Then he recited the following *ayat*:

**Those of the Tribe of Israel who disbelieved were cursed by the tongue of Da'ud and of 'Isa son of Maryam – that is because they rebelled and exceeded the limits.**

> **They did not forbid each other the wrong they were doing – and what they used to do was certainly awful.**
>
> **You will see many of them making friends with those who disbelieve – and what they have prepared for themselves is certainly awful: for them to have incurred the anger of Allah on themselves and to live in punishment for ever.**
>
> **And if they had believed in Allah and in the Prophet and in what has been revealed to him, they would not take them as friends, but many of them are evil livers. (5.78-81).**

Then he said, 'Indeed! – I swear by Allah, you must command what is good and forbid what is evil, and stop whoever does wrong, and make him do what is right, and restrict him to what is permitted!' (Abu Da'ud).

Allah says in the *ayah* which follows:

> **You will certainly find that the most implacable of people in their enmity towards those who believe are the Jews and those who worship idols, and you will certainly find that the nearest in their affection towards those who trust are those who say, 'Surely we are Christians'. That is because there are priests and monks among them, and because they are not proud. (5.82).**

## THE CHRISTIANS

As we have just seen, in describing the Christians Allah says:

> **You will certainly find that the most implacable of people in their enmity towards those who believe are the Jews and those who worship idols, and you will certainly find that the nearest in their affection towards those who trust are those who say, 'Surely we are Christians'. That is because there are priests and monks among them, and because they are not proud.**

**And when they listen to what has been revealed to the Messenger, you see their eyes fill with tears as they recognise the truth. They say, 'Our Lord, we believe – so record us as being among those who bear witness.**

**'And how can we not believe in Allah and in what has come to us of the truth – and (how can we not) hope that our Lord will lead us in (to the Garden) with the people who are righteous?'**

**And Allah has rewarded them for what they say, with Gardens underneath which rivers flow, in which they shall dwell for ever – and that is the reward for those who do good.**

**And as for those who disbelieve and deny Our signs – these are the people of Hell. (5.82-86).**

Whereas Allah severely reprimands the Jews for deliberately concealing and changing what was originally revealed to *sayyedina* Musa, peace be on him, as regards the Christians He simply points out that they have forgotten part of what was originally revealed to *sayyedina* 'Isa, peace be on him:

**And We made a covenant with those who say, 'Surely we are Christians,' but they forgot a part of what they had been reminded – so We have stirred up enmity and hatred among them until the Day of Standing, when Allah will show them what they were doing. (5.14).**

It is clear from the Qur'an, however, that those Christians who refuse to accept Islam are more closely allied with the Jews than with the Muslims, and Allah warns the Muslims not to take them as their friends:

**And the Jews will not be pleased with you, and neither will the Christians, until you follow their system. Say: 'Surely the guidance of Allah is the only guidance.' And if you were to follow their desires, after the knowledge which has**

**come to you, you would not have in Allah any friend or helper.**

**Those to whom We have given the Book and who read it as it should be read, these believe in it – and as for whoever rejects it, then these are the losers. (2.120-121).**

And:

**O you who believe, do not take the Jews and the Christians as friends – they are friends to one another – and whoever of you makes friends with them is surely one of them. Surely Allah does not guide people who are wrong doers.**

**And you see those in whose hearts there is a sickness going hastily over to them, saying, 'We are afraid that we are going to suffer a change of fortune.'**

**And it may be that Allah will grant (you) victory, or a decree directly from Him, so that they may feel remorse about what they secretly kept to themselves.**

**And then those who believe will say, 'Are these the ones who swore by Allah their most binding oaths that they were surely with you?' – Their actions have proved fruitless, and they have become losers. (5.51-53)**

And:

**O you who believe, do not make friends with those from among those who were given the Book before you, and from among the disbelievers, who treat your *deen* as a joke and a game. And have *taqwa* of Allah, if you are indeed believers.**

**And when you call (them) to the prayer, they treat it as a joke and a game – that is because they are a people who lack understanding. (5.57-58).**

And:

**O you who believe, do not make close friends with those who are not like you – who will not stop trying to corrupt you and who would love to destroy you.**

**Their hatred is indeed apparent from what they say, but what their hearts conceal is worse – We have indeed made the signs clear to you, if you have any intellect.**

**Although you are the ones who love them, they do not love you – and you believe in all of the Book.**

**And when they meet you, they say, 'We believe,' – but when they are alone, they bite their finger-tips in their rage at you.**

**Say: 'May you die with rage!'**

**Surely Allah knows what is hidden in your hearts.**

**If good comes to you it grieves them, and if bad strikes you it makes them glad, but if you are patient and have *taqwa*, then their cunning will not harm you at all – surely Allah encompasses whatever they are doing.** (3.118-120).

It is clear from the Qur'an that the main error of the Christians has been to elevate *sayyedina* 'Isa, peace be on him, far beyond his station as a Prophet and a Messenger, by mistakenly making him the 'son' of God:

**And they say, 'Allah has chosen a son.' Glory be to Him! Indeed whatever is in the heavens and the earth is His. Everything is subservient to Him, the Bringer into Being of the heavens and the earth – and when He decrees a matter, then all He says to it is 'Be!' and it is.** (2.116-117).

And:

**Those who say, 'Surely Allah is the Messiah, son of Maryam,' have indeed disbelieved.**

Say: 'And who would have any power at all over Allah if He wished to destroy the Messiah son of Maryam, and his mother, and whoever is on earth, all together? And dominion over the heavens and the earth and what is between them belongs to Allah – He creates what He wants – and Allah has power over everything.

And the Jews and the Christians say, 'We are sons of Allah and His loved ones.'

Say: 'Then why does He punish you for your wrong actions?'

You are certainly human beings whom He has created. He forgives whomever He wishes, and He punishes whomever He wishes, and dominion over the heavens and the earth and what is between them belongs to Allah – and the journeying is to Him. (5.17-18).

And:

Those who say, 'Surely Allah is the Messiah, son of Mary,' are certainly disbelievers.

And the Messiah said: 'O Tribe of Israel, worship Allah, my Lord and your Lord. As for whoever associates partners with Allah, surely Allah has certainly forbidden him the Garden and his abode will be the Fire – and for the wrong doers there will be no helpers.'

Those who say, 'Surely Allah is one of three in a trinity,' are certainly disbelievers – for there is no god except the One God.

And if they do not desist from what they are saying, a painful punishment will certainly befall those of them who disbelieve.

Will they not rather turn to Allah in repentance and seek His forgiveness? And Allah is Forgiving, Compassionate. (5.72-74).

And:

**O People of the Book, do not go to extremes in your religion, and do not say anything about Allah except the truth.**

**Surely the Messiah 'Isa son of Maryam was a Messenger of Allah, and His Word which He sent down into Maryam, and a Spirit from Him – so believe in Allah and His messengers, and do not say, 'Three.' Stop it! (That would be) better for you. Surely Allah is only One God!**

**Glory be to Him – far beyond His having a son – when what is in the heavens and what is in the earth is His. – And Allah is enough to look after it.** (4.171).

And:

**Allah has not chosen any son, and there is not any other god as well as Him – otherwise each god would certainly have taken over what it had created, and some would have exalted themselves over others.**

**Glory be to Allah above what they assert – the Knower of the Unseen and the Seen, may He be exalted far above the partners they associate with Him!** (23.91-92).

And:

**Surely the *deen* is only for Allah.**

**And those who choose guardians other than Him (say), 'We only worship them so that they will bring us nearer to Allah.' – Surely Allah will judge between them concerning what they used to disagree about. Surely Allah does not guide whoever denies in disbelief.**

**If Allah had wanted to have a son, He could certainly have chosen whatever He wanted from His creation – Glory be to Him! He is Allah, the One, the Compeller!** (39.3-4).

And:

> **Say: 'If the Merciful did have a son, then I would be the foremost of the worshippers.'**
>
> **Glory be to the Lord of the heavens and the earth, the Lord of the Throne, above what they assert. (43.81-82).**

And:

> **And certainly if you ask them, 'Who created the heavens and the earth?' they will certainly say, 'Allah.'**
>
> **Say: 'Do you not see, regarding whatever you pray to instead of Allah, that if Allah wished to harm me, how could they protect me from His harm – or if He wished to show mercy to me, how could they withhold His mercy?'**
>
> **Say: 'Allah is enough for me – in Him do those who trust put their trust.' (39.38).**

And:

> **Say: 'Are you telling me to worship other than Allah? – You fools!' (39.64).**

And:

> **Blessed is the One Who has revealed the Discrimination (between right and wrong) to His slave (Muhammad), so that he might be a warner to all the worlds – the One to Whom the dominion of the heavens and the earth belongs – and He has not chosen a son, and He does not have any partner to share the dominion, and He has created everything and determined its destiny. – And yet they have chosen gods instead of Him who cannot create anything but are themselves created, and who do not have any power either to harm or to benefit themselves, and who do not have any power over either death, or life, or raising the dead! (25.1-3).**

And:

**And they say, 'The Merciful has chosen a son.'**

**You have indeed come up with something terrible – so that the heavens are almost torn apart, and the earth split open, and the mountains scattered in pieces – that you should claim that the Merciful has a son!**

**And it is not in the nature of things for the Merciful to choose a son – when every one in the heavens and the earth only comes to the Merciful as a slave.**

**He certainly knows them all – and He knows their number exactly – and each of them will come to Him on the Day of Standing, alone.** (19.88-95).

And:

**And We did not send any Messenger in the past without inspiring in him, 'Surely there is no god except Me – so worship Me.'**

**And they say, 'The Merciful has chosen a son.'**

**Glory be to Him! – They are only slaves who have been honoured:**

**They do not speak before He has spoken, and what they do is by His command.**

**He knows what is ahead of them and what is behind them, and they cannot intercede except on behalf of whomever is pleasing to Him, and they tremble in fear of Him.**

**And if one of them were to say, 'Surely I am God and not Him,' then we would repay anyone like that with Hell – that is how We reward wrong doers.** (21.25-29).

And:

**They say: 'Allah has chosen a son.' – Glory be to Him! – He is the Self-Sufficient! Whatever is in the heavens and whatever is in the earth belongs to Him. You do not have any authority for (saying) this. Why do you say things about Allah of which you have no knowledge?**

**Say: 'Surely those who make up a lie about Allah will not be successful.'**

**They will pass their time in this world, and then to Us they will return, and then We will make them taste intense punishment because they used to disbelieve. (10.68-70).**

Thus in the opening *ayat* of Surat al-Kahf, Allah states that one of the reasons why the Qur'an has been revealed is to warn those who claim that Allah has a son:

**In the Name of Allah the Merciful the Compassionate**

**Praise belongs to Allah Who has revealed the Book to His slave (Muhammad).**

**And He has not put any distortion in it, only clarity, in order to warn of a severe punishment from Him, and to give good news to the believers who do good that theirs will be a good reward, where they will dwell for ever, and to warn those who say, 'Allah has chosen a son,' which is something they know nothing about, and neither did their fathers.**

**The words which they utter are dreadful – surely what they say is nothing but a lie. (18.1-5).**

For:

**It is not how it is for Allah to choose any son. – Glory be to Him! – When He decrees a matter, then all He says to it is 'Be!' and it is. (19.35).**

And:

**O mankind, a simile is coined for you – so pay attention to it: Surely those to whom you pray instead of Allah could never create a fly, even if they all tried together – and if the fly took something from them, they could not retrieve it from it: How weak are both the seeker and the sought!** (22.73).

Accordingly, Allah tells the Muslims what to say to those Christians who seek to argue with them about *sayyedina* 'Isa, peace be on him:

**Surely the similarity of 'Isa with Allah is like the similarity of Adam. – He created him from dust, and then said to him: 'Be!' and he is.**

**This is the truth from your Lord, so do not be one of those who doubt.**

**And as for whoever argues with you about him ('Isa), after the knowledge which has come to you, then say: 'Come, let us summon our sons and your sons, and our women and your women, and ourselves and yourselves – and then let us humbly pray, and invoke the curse of Allah upon those who lie.'** (3.59-61).

It is interesting, as regards these last *ayat*, to consider the following passage from *Ash-Shifa'* of *Qadi* 'Iyad, which is taken from the section which considers the inimitability of the Qur'an and in which there is a description of what happened when the Christian bishops of Najran, in Yemen, came to Madina to visit *sayyedina* Muhammad, may Allah bless him and grant him peace, in 10 AH:

When the bishops of Najran came to him and refused Islam, Allah sent down the *ayah* of the mutual curse on them saying, **'Whoever disputes with you about him (i.e. 'Isa) after the knowledge that has come to you, say: "Come now, let us call on our sons and your sons, our wives and your wives, our selves and your selves, then let us humbly pray and lay the curse of Allah on those who lie."'** (3:61).

> They were stopped from doing that and were content to pay the *jizya* tax. That is because al-'Aqib, their leader, told them, "You know that he is a Prophet. A Prophet never lays a curse on a people but that neither their small or great survive."
>
> It is the same when Allah says, **'If you are in doubt about what We have sent down on Our slave then bring a *surah* like it and call upon your witnesses, apart from Allah, if you are truthful. If you do not, and you will not, then fear the Fire whose fuel is men and stones, prepared for the unbelievers.' (2:24).**
>
> Allah told the Arabs that they would not do it and indeed they did not. This *ayah* is one of the reports about the unseen, but it still contains their incapacity to respond to the challenge at the beginning of the *ayah*. (*Ash-Shifa* of *Qadi* 'Iyad: 1.4.8).

From the time of the Prophet Muhammad, may Allah bless him and grant him peace, up to the present day, no Jew has longed for death, no Christian has invoked the mutual curse, and no one has been able to compose a *surah* like one of the *surahs* of the Qur'an, of which the smallest, Surat al-Kawthar, only has ten words.

## THE PEOPLE OF THE BOOK

When addressing the People of the Book Allah says:

> **O you to whom the Book has been given, believe in what We have revealed – confirming what you already have from before – before We obliterate appearances and turn them upside down, or curse them just as We cursed those who broke the sabbath – and Allah's command is always carried out.**
>
> **Surely Allah does not forgive partners being associated with Him, but He forgives whomever He wishes anything other than that – and whoever associates partners with Allah has certainly conceived a tremendous sin.**

Have you not seen those who claim to be purifying themselves? Indeed – but it is Allah Who purifies whomever He wishes – and they will not be wronged (even as much as) the skin of a date-stone.

See how they make up lies about Allah! – And that in itself is clearly a sin.

Have you not seen how those who have been given part of the Book believe in idols and false gods – and how they say of those who reject, 'These ones are more rightly-guided along the way than those who believe'?

These are the ones whom Allah has cursed – and as for whomever Allah has cursed, you will never find any helper for him.

Do they have part of the dominion? – Then in that case they would not give people (even as much as) the speck on a date-stone.

Or are they jealous of people because of what Allah has given them out of His generosity? – For We indeed gave the people of Ibrahim the Book and the wisdom, and We gave them a mighty kingdom.

And from among them were those who believed in it, and from among them were those who turned away from it – and Hell will be enough for burning them.

As for those who reject Our signs, surely We shall burn them in the Fire – as often as their skin is consumed, We shall replace it with another skin, so that they taste the torment again – surely Allah is always Mighty, Wise.

And as for those who believe and do good, We shall make them enter Gardens underneath which rivers flow, in which they will dwell for ever, in which they will have pure companions – and We shall make them enter in abundant shade. (4.47-57).

In describing the Fire, Allah confirms that there are nineteen angels in charge of it – a fact of which only those who have access to the earlier revelations such as the Taurah and the Ingil would be aware:

> **And what can tell you what the Fire of Hell is like?**
>
> **It does not leave anything untouched and it does not leave anything alone and it chars people black.**
>
> **There are nineteen in charge of it – and We have put only angels in charge of the Fire – and the number We have chosen is only as a test for those who disbelieve, and so that it may add to the certainty of those who were given the Book (in the past) and increase the belief of those who believe, and so that those who were given the Book (in the past) and the believers will not be in any doubt, and so that those in whose hearts there is a sickness and the disbelievers will say, 'What does Allah mean by this example?'**
>
> **That is how Allah leads astray whomever He wishes and guides whomever He wishes – and no one except Him knows the forces of your Lord – and this is nothing but a reminder to people. (74.27-31).**

Allah promises those among the People of the Book who are sincere in their actions that they will have nothing to fear:

> **Surely those who believe and those who are Jews and the Sabaeans and the Christians – whoever believes in Allah and the Last Day and does good – they shall not be afraid and they shall not be sad. (5.69).**

And that they will receive their due:

> **Surely those who believe and those who are Jews and the Christians and the Sabaeans – whoever believes in Allah and the Last Day and does good – surely their reward is with their Lord and they shall not be afraid and they shall not be sad. (2.62).**

And that Allah will judge between them on the Last Day:

> **Surely those who believe and those who are Jews and the Sabaeans and the Christians and the Magians and those who worship idols – surely Allah will judge between them on the Day of Standing; surely Allah is Witness of every thing.** (22.17).

Again, when addressing the Muslims, Allah says:

> **You are the best community that has been raised up for mankind, commanding what is good and forbidding what is bad and believing in Allah.**
>
> **And if only the People of the Book had believed, it would certainly have been better for them. Some of them are believers, but most of them are evil livers.**
>
> **They will not harm you except for a little annoyance, and if they fight against you they will turn their backs on you and flee – and then they will not be helped.**
>
> **They will be stamped with humiliation wherever they are found, except when they have a covenant with Allah and a covenant with people – for they have incurred the anger of Allah and so poverty will be stamped on them – that is because they rejected the signs of Allah and killed the Prophets without any justification. That is because they rebelled and were wicked.**
>
> **They are not all alike. There is an upright community of the People of the Book who recite the revelations of Allah in the night time and who prostrate themselves (before Him). They believe in Allah and the Last Day, and they command what is right and forbid what is wrong, and they are swift to do good – and these are among the righteous, and as for whatever good they do, none of it will be rejected.**
>
> **And Allah knows those who have *taqwa*.** (3.110-115).

And:

**And surely among the People of the Book there are some who believe in Allah and in what has been revealed to you and in what has been revealed to them – humble before Allah, they do not exchange the signs of Allah for something of little value. As for them, their reward is with their Lord – surely Allah is swift at the reckoning.** (3.199).

And:

**As for those to whom We gave the Book before it (the Qur'an), they believe in it, and when it is recited to them they say, 'We believe in it – surely it is the truth from our Lord – surely even before it we were Muslims.'**

**These will be given their reward twice over – because they are patient, and they repel evil with good, and they spend from what We have provided for them, and when they hear idle talk they turn away from it and say, 'To us our actions, and to you your actions – peace on you – we do not want to be among those who are ignorant.'** (28.52-55).

And:

**O you who believe, have *taqwa* of Allah and believe in His Messenger (Muhammad), and He will give you a double taste of His mercy, and He will give you a light in which to walk, and He will forgive you – and Allah is Forgiving, Compassionate – so that the People of the Book may know that they do not have any control over any of the generosity of Allah, and that generosity is in Allah's hand to give to whomever He wishes – and Allah's generosity is vast.** (57.28-29).

And:

**And those to whom We have given the Book rejoice in what has been revealed to you (Muhammad) – and from among the clans there are those who deny some of it.**

**Say: 'Surely I am commanded to worship Allah only and not to associate any partner with Him – to Him I pray and to Him is my return.' (13.36).**

And:

**And do not argue with the People of the Book – except for those of them who do wrong – unless it is with what is best, and say, 'We believe in what has been revealed to us and in what has been revealed to you – and our God and your God is One, and it is to Him that we submit.'**

**And We have revealed the Book to you in this way, and those to whom We gave the Book (in the past) believe in it – and from among these others there are some who believe in it – and no one opposes Our signs except those who disbelieve. (29.46-47).**

It is clear from the following *ayat*, however, that not all of the Jews and the Christians have the same attitude or degree of understanding:

**And they say, 'No one will enter the Garden except whoever is a Jew or a Christian.'**

**This is what they want.**

**Say: 'Show your proof, if you are speaking the truth.'**

**Indeed, for whoever submits his will to Allah while doing good, then his reward is with his Lord – and they shall not be afraid and they shall not be sad.**

**And the Jews say, 'The Christians do not have anything,' and the Christians say, 'The Jews do not have anything,' – and they both recite the Book!**

**That is how those who do not know speak – and Allah will judge between them, concerning what they used to disagree about, on the Day of Standing. (2.111-113).**

And:

> **And they say, 'Be Jews or Christians,' and you will be rightly guided.**
>
> **Say: 'No, rather the way of Ibrahim, the *hanif* – and he was not one of the idol worshippers.'**
>
> **Say: 'We believe in Allah and in what has been revealed to us and in what was revealed to Ibrahim and to Isma'il and to Ishaq and to Ya'qub and to the tribes (of Israel), and in what Musa and 'Isa were given and in what the Prophets received from their Lord; we make no distinction between any of them, and to Him we have surrendered.'**
>
> **And if they believe in the like of what you believe in, then they are rightly guided; and if they turn away, then they have separated; and Allah is enough for you; and He is the Hearer, the Knower.**
>
> **'(We take our) colour from Allah – and who is better than Allah at giving colour? – and we are His worshippers.'**
>
> **Say: 'Are you going to argue with us about Allah, when He is our Lord and your Lord? We have our actions, and you have your actions, and we are being sincere to Him – or do you say that Ibrahim and Isma'il and Ishaq and Ya'qub and the tribes (of Israel) were Jews or Christians?'**
>
> **Say: 'Do you know best, or does Allah?'**
>
> **And who is more in the dark than whoever conceals a testimony which he has from Allah? – And Allah does not forget about what you were doing.**
>
> **That was a nation that has passed away – they will have what they earned, and you will have what you have earned, and you will not be asked about what they used to do. (2.135-141).**

Allah makes it clear that He can forgive anything except *shirk*, which is worshipping other than Him instead of Him:

> **Surely Allah does not forgive partners being associated with Him, but He forgives whomever He wishes anything other than that – and whoever associates partners with Allah has certainly gone far astray. (4.116).**

And Allah makes it clear that it is He Who decides who is for the Fire and who is for the Garden:

> **And as for those who believe and do good, We shall bring them into Gardens underneath which rivers flow, in which they will dwell for ever.**
>
> **It is a promise from Allah which is true, and who can be more truthful than Allah in what is said?**
>
> **It will not be as you wish, and it will not be as the People of the Book wish:**
>
> **Whoever does evil will receive its reward – and will not find any friend or any helper other than Allah.**
>
> **And whoever does good – whether male or female – and is a believer, then they will enter the Garden, and they will not be wronged (even as much as) the speck on a date-stone.**
>
> **And who is better in their *deen* than whoever submits their will to Allah while doing good and follows the way of Ibrahim, the *hanif*? – And Allah chose Ibrahim as an intimate friend.**
>
> **And whatever is in the heavens and whatever is in the earth belongs to Allah – and Allah is always encompassing everything. (4.122-126).**

Thus the Qur'an makes it clear that the Muslims are those who believe not only in *sayyedina* Muhammad, may Allah bless him and grant him peace, but also in all the Prophets who came before him, may the blessings and peace of Allah be on all of them – and in the One Who sent them:

**Say: 'O People of the Book, let us come to an agreement between us and you: that we shall worship none but Allah, and that we shall not associate any partner with Him, and that none of us shall take others for lords instead of Allah.'**

**And if they turn away, then say: 'Bear witness that we are Muslims.'**

**O People of the Book, why do you argue about Ibrahim, when the Taurah and the Ingil were not revealed until after him? Have you no intellect?**

**You certainly argue about what you have some knowledge about, but why argue about what you have no knowledge about? – And Allah knows, and you do not know.**

**Ibrahim was not a Jew, and he was not a Christian, but he was *hanif* – a Muslim – and he was not one of those who worship idols.**

**Surely the people who are closest to Ibrahim are those who followed him, and this Prophet (Muhammad), and those who believe – and Allah is the Friend of the believers.**

**A party of the People of the Book would love to lead you astray – but they do not lead anyone astray except themselves, although they do not perceive this.**

**O People of the Book, why do you reject the signs of Allah, when you witness them?**

**O People of the Book, why do you cover up the truth with falsehood and knowingly conceal the truth?**

**And a party of the People of the Book say, 'Believe in what has been revealed to those who believe at the start of the day, and then at its end reject it, so that perhaps they may**

**return (to disbelief) – and do not believe anyone except whoever follows your own religion.'**

**Say: 'Surely Allah's guidance is the guidance – whether (or not) anyone is given the like of what you were given, and whether (or not) they argue with you in the presence of your Lord.'**

**Say: 'Surely generosity is in Allah's hand – He gives it to whomever He wants – and Allah is Immense, Knowing. He chooses whomever He wishes for His mercy – and Allah's generosity is vast.'**

**And from among the People of the Book there is the one who, if you entrust him with a *qintar*, will return it to you – and from among them is the one who, if you entrust him with a *dinar*, will not return it to you unless you keep on asking him for it.**

**That is because they say, 'We have no obligation towards the *goyim*,' – and this, which they say is from Allah, is a lie, and they know it.**

**Indeed – and as for whoever keeps his promise and has *taqwa*, then surely Allah loves those who have *taqwa*.**

**As for those who exchange their covenant with Allah and the promises they have made for a small gain – surely they will have no share of good in the next world, and Allah will not speak to them and He will not look at them on the Day of Standing, and He will not purify them – and theirs will be a painful punishment.**

**And surely there is certainly a group of them who distort what is in the Book with what they say, so as to make you think that it is from the Book when it is not from the Book – and they say, 'This is from Allah,' when it is not from Allah – and this, which they say is from Allah, is a lie, and they know it.**

It is not possible for any man to whom Allah has given the Book and wisdom and prophethood to then say to people, 'Worship me instead of Allah,' but only, 'Worship your Lord – by your spreading knowledge of the Book, and by your studying it.'

And he did not command you to take the angels and the Prophets as your lords – would he command you to disbelief after you had become Muslims?

And when Allah made His covenant with the Prophets, (He said), 'This is what I have given you as a Book and wisdom, and then a Messenger (Muhammad) will come to you confirming what you have – and you will believe in him and you will help him.'

He said, 'Will you be bound by this and will you accept this obligation?'

They replied, 'We will be bound by it.'

He said, 'Then bear witness to it – and I will bear witness with you – and as for whoever turns away after this, then they will be the ones who disobey.'

Do they desire other than the *deen* of Allah, when whatever is in the heavens or the earth submits to Him, willingly or unwillingly, and to Him they will return?

Say: 'We believe in Allah, and in what has been revealed to us, and in what was revealed to Ibrahim and to Isma'il and to Ishaq and to Ya'qub and to the tribes (of Israel), and in what was given to Musa and 'Isa and the Prophets from their Lord – we make no distinction between any of them, and to Him we have submitted.'

And as for whoever desires a life transaction other than Islam, it will not be accepted from him, and in the next life he will be among the losers.

**How can Allah guide a people who disbelieved after they had believed and had borne witness that the Messenger was true, and after clear proofs had come to them? – And Allah does not guide wrong doing people.**

**As for them, their reward is that the curse of Allah and of the angels and of all mankind is on them – under that they will abide for ever – and their punishment will not be eased, and they will not be reprieved, except for those who turn in repentance after that and do good – for surely Allah is Forgiving, Merciful. (3.64-89).**

The Qur'an also makes it clear that some of the People of the Book prefer their falsehood to the truth, even though they know that their teachings have been altered and that the teaching of *sayyedina* Muhammad is pure:

**And when a Messenger (Muhammad) comes to them from Allah confirming what they already have, a party of those who have been given the Book hide the Book of Allah behind their backs as if they did not know about it, and follow what the *shayatin* taught during the reign of Sulayman – and Sulayman did not disbelieve, but it was the *shayatin* who disbelieved, teaching people magic and what was revealed to the two angels in Babel – Harut and Marut – and they did not teach it to anyone until they had said, 'Surely we are only a test, so do not disbelieve.'**

**And from these two they have learned how to cause separation between a man and his wife – and they cannot harm anyone with it except by the permission of Allah – and they have only learned what is harmful for them, and not what is beneficial for them; and they certainly know that whoever deals in it will not have any share of good in the next life, and certainly what they have sold their selves for is awful – if only they knew.**

**And if only they had believed and had *taqwa*, their reward from Allah would certainly have been better – if only they knew. (2.101-103).**

(The meaning of the above passage is open to more than one interpretation. *Qadi* 'Iyad's commentary on it is quoted in Chapter Four, on pages 79-81.)

And:

**And (remember) when Allah made a covenant with those who were given the Book to, 'Make it clear to people, and do not conceal it,' but they hid it behind their backs and exchanged it for something of little value – and what they have in exchange is awful.**

**Do not think that those who exult in what they have given and who love to be praised for what they have not done – do not think that they are safe from punishment – and theirs will be a painful punishment.**

**And the dominion of the heavens and the earth belongs to Allah – and Allah has power over everything. (3.187-189).**

And:

**Neither those who reject from among the People of the Book nor the idol worshippers like anything good to be revealed to you from your Lord, but Allah chooses whomever He wishes for His mercy – and Allah's generosity is vast. (2.105).**

And:

**Do you not know that it is Allah Who has dominion over the heavens and the earth – and that you do not have any friend or any helper other than Allah?**

**Do you want to question your Messenger as Musa was questioned in the past?**

**And whoever exchanges disbelief for belief has indeed gone astray from the right way.**

**And many of the People of the Book would love to turn you back into disbelievers after your belief, out of the envy in their selves, after the truth has been made clear to them, but forgive them and pardon them, until the command of Allah comes to pass – surely Allah has power over everything. (2.107-109).**

And:

**Do you not see that those who have been given part of the Book have exchanged it for going astray, and that they want you also to go astray from the way?**

**And Allah knows best who your enemies are – and Allah is enough as a Guardian, and Allah is enough as a Helper. (4.44-45).**

And, in the *ayat* which commanded the Prophet Muhammad, may Allah bless him and grant him peace, to change the direction in which the Muslims face when doing the prayer, from Jerusalem to Makka:

**We have indeed seen you turning your face to heaven – and now We will certainly make you turn towards a *qibla* which is pleasing to you – so turn your face towards the Sacred Mosque (in Makka), and wherever you may be, turn your faces towards it. And surely those who have been given the Book certainly know that this is the truth from their Lord – and Allah is not unaware of what they are doing. And even if you brought all kinds of signs to those who have been given the Book, they would not follow your *qibla* – and you will never follow their *qibla*, and they will never follow each other's *qibla* – and if you were to follow their desires after the knowledge which has come to you, then surely you would certainly be among the wrong doers.**

**Those who have been given the Book recognise this just as they recognise their own sons – but surely a party of them knowingly conceal the truth.**

**The truth is from your Lord – so do not be among those who doubt. (2.144-147).**

And:

**Those who have been given the Book recognise this just as they recognise their own sons – but they deceive themselves and so they will not believe. (6.20).**

And:

**Say: 'O People of the Book, why do you reject the signs of Allah when (you know that) Allah is witnessing what you are doing?'**

**Say: 'O you who believe, if you were to obey a group of those who were given the Book, they would make you become disbelievers again after your belief.'**

**And how can you disbelieve, when the signs of Allah are recited to you and His Messenger is among you?**

**And whoever holds on firmly to Allah will indeed be guided on a straight path.**

**O you who believe, have *taqwa* of Allah with the *taqwa* which is due to Him, and do not die except as Muslims. (3.98-102).**

Allah tells the followers of *sayyedina* Muhammad what to say to those from among the People of the Book who are bitterly opposed to the Muslims:

**Say: 'O People of the Book, do you reject us just because we believe in Allah, and in what has been revealed to us, and in what was revealed in the past, and because most of you are evil livers?'**

**Say: 'Shall I tell you what is worse than that as far as retribution from Allah is concerned? It is for whomever Allah**

has cursed and is angry with – and whomever of these He has turned into apes and pigs – and whoever worships false gods. These are in a worse situation and are further astray from the right way.'

And when they come to you, they say, 'We believe,' – when in fact they came in not believing and they certainly left the same – and Allah knows best what they were concealing.

And you see many of them competing with each other in wickedness and enmity and devouring what is forbidden – what they are doing is certainly awful.

Why do the rabbis and the priests not forbid their evil words and their devouring what is forbidden? What they are doing is certainly awful. (5.59-63).

And:

And the Jews say, 'Ezra is the son of Allah,' and the Christians say, 'The Messiah is the son of Allah.'

These are the words that they utter, which are like the words of those who disbelieved in the past – Allah curse them – what liars they are!

They have taken their rabbis and their monks as their lords instead of Allah – and the Messiah son of Maryam – and they were commanded only to worship One God. There is no god except Him. Glory be to Him, above what they associate with Him.

They want to put out the Light of Allah with their mouths, but Allah seeks only to perfect His Light, however much those who reject may detest it.

He is the One who has sent His Messenger with guidance and the true *deen* so that it may overcome all other *deens*, however much those who worship idols may detest it.

> **Oh you who believe, surely many of the rabbis and the monks certainly devour the wealth of people through deception and lead them away from the way of Allah. And as for those who hoard up gold and silver and do not spend it in the way of Allah, tell them of a painful punishment – on a Day when it will be heated up in the Fire of Hell, and then their foreheads and their sides and their backs will be branded with it, (and they will be told), 'This is what you used to hoard up for yourselves – so have a taste of what you used to hoard!' (9.30-35).**

And Allah tells the followers of *sayyedina* Muhammad how to treat those from among the People of the Book who are opposed to the Muslims:

> **Fight those from among those who have been given the Book who do not believe in Allah or in the Last Day, and who do not forbid what Allah and His Messenger have forbidden, and who do not follow the true *deen* – until they pay the *jizya* of their own accord, after they have been subdued. (9.29).**

In spite of their opposition to *sayyedina* Muhammad, may Allah bless him and grant him peace, and the Qur'an, Allah invites all of the People of the Book in every age to follow him:

> **O People of the Book, now has Our Messenger indeed come to you, making clear to you much of what you used to hide in the Book, and forgiving much. Now there has indeed come to you from Allah a Light and a clear Book, whereby Allah guides whoever seeks His pleasure to paths of peace – and He brings them out of darkness into light by His decree, and guides them to a straight path. (5.15-16).**

And:

> **O People of the Book, now has Our Messenger indeed come to you to make things clear to you after an interval between Messengers, lest you should say, 'Neither a bringer of good news nor a warner ever came to us.'**

**And now a bringer of good news and a warner has indeed come to you – and Allah has power over everything. (5.19).**

Allah also says in the Qur'an:

**In the Name of Allah the Merciful the Compassionate**

**Those who disbelieve from among the People of the Book and those who worship idols could not have ceased (doing so) until clear proof came to them:**

**A Messenger from Allah, reciting from a Book free from impurity containing true revelations.**

**And the People who were given the Book did not become divided until after clear proof came to them, and they were not commanded (to do) anything other than to worship Allah, sincere to Him in their *deen – hanif* – and to establish the prayer and to pay the *zakat* – and that is the true *deen*.**

**Surely those who disbelieve from among the People of the Book and those who worship idols will abide in the Fire of Hell for ever. They are the worst of created beings.**

**Surely those who trust and do good are the best of created beings. Their reward is with their Lord – Gardens of Eden underneath which rivers flow, in which they will dwell for ever. Allah is pleased with them and they are pleased with Him. – This is for whoever fears his Lord. (98.1-8).**

And:

**Whoever purifies his self, and remembers the Name of his Lord, and does the prayer, is indeed successful – but you prefer the life of this world, even though the next life is better and more lasting!**

**Surely this is certainly in the earlier Books, the Books of Ibrahim and Musa. (87.14-19).**

Again, in Surah al-Mai'dah, Allah reminds the People of the Book of the reward that awaits those who follow *sayyedina* Muhammad, may Allah bless him and grant him peace – the same reward which awaits whoever has truly followed not only *sayyedina* Musa and *sayyedina* 'Isa, but all of the Prophets and Messengers who came before and after them, may the blessings and peace of Allah be on all of them:

**And if only the People of the Book would trust and have *taqwa*, We would certainly remit their sins for them, and We would certainly bring them into Gardens of Delight.**

**And if they had only followed the Taurah and the Ingil and what was revealed to them from their Lord, they would certainly have been nourished from above them and from beneath their feet. Among them there is a community who are on the right path – but what many of them do is evil. (5.65-66).**

And:

**Say: 'O People of the Book, you will not have anything until you follow the Taurah and the Injil and what has been revealed to you from your Lord.'**

**And what has been revealed to you from your Lord is certain to increase the disobedience and disbelief of many of them – but do not feel sorry for people who are disbelievers. (5.68).**

And:

**Say: 'O People of the Book, do not emphasise anything other than the truth in your religion, and do not follow the desires of people who certainly went astray in the past, and who led many astray, and who went astray from the right way.' (5.77).**

And:

**Surely the *deen* with Allah is Islam.**

**And those who were given the Book (in the past) did not disagree until after knowledge had come to them, out of rivalry amongst themselves – and as for whoever rejects the signs of Allah, then surely Allah is swift at the reckoning.**

**And if they argue with you, then say, 'I have submitted my will to Allah – together with whoever follows me.'**

**And say to those who were given the Book (in the past) and to those who are illiterate, 'Have you submitted?'**

**And if they have submitted then they are indeed rightly guided, and if they turn away then it is only up to you to deliver the message – and Allah is All-Seeing over (His) slaves.**

**As for those who reject the signs of Allah, and who kill the Prophets without any justification, and who kill those people who demand justice – tell them of a painful punishment.**

**These are the ones whose actions have failed both in this world and in the next world – and they will not have any helpers.**

**Have you not seen how those who have been given part of the Book invoke the Book of Allah to reach a judgement between them – and then a group of them turn away in disagreement?**

**That is because they say, 'The Fire will not touch us except for a certain number of days,' – and so what they used to make up in their religion has deceived them.**

**How will it be when We have gathered them all together on a Day about which there is no doubt, when every self will be paid in full for what it has earned – and they will not be wronged? (3.19-25).**

And:

**And the different groups among them disagree with each other – so woe to those who disbelieve in the meeting on a mighty Day: listen to them, and look, on the Day they meet Us! – and today the wrong doers are clearly astray, so warn them about the Day of regret when the matter will be judged, for now they are careless and they do not believe.**

**Surely it is We Who will inherit the earth and whatever is in it – and it is to Us they will return. (19.37-40).**

And:

**And what will tell you what the Day of Judgement is? Again – what will tell you what the Day of Judgement is? A Day on which no one has any power over any one else at all – on that Day the affair will belong entirely to Allah. (82.17-19).**

And:

**Say: 'O Allah, the King Who has the dominion, You give power to whomever You wish and You take away power from whomever You wish; and You exalt whomever You wish and You humiliate whomever You wish – good is in Your hand – surely You have power over everything.**

**'You make the night turn into the day and You make the day turn into the night; and You bring out the living from the dead and You bring out the dead from the living – and You provide for whomever You wish without calculating. (3.26-27).**

And:

**In the Name of Allah the Merciful the Compassionate**

**Say: 'He is Allah the One – Allah the Everlasting – no one is born from Him and He is not born from anything – and there is nothing like Him.' (112.1-4).**

It has been transmitted by Abu Hurayra, may Allah be pleased with him, that the Prophet Muhammad, may Allah bless him and grant him peace, said, ' By Him in Whose hand is the life of Muhammad, whoever of the Jews or Christians hears about me, but does not affirm belief in what I have been sent with (the Qur'an), and dies in this state, will be one of the inhabitants of the Fire of Hell.' (Muslim).

It has been transmitted by Abu Musa al-Ash'ari, may Allah be pleased with him, that the Prophet Muhammad, may Allah bless him and grant him peace, said, 'If anyone believes in 'Isa ibn Maryam and then believes in me, then he will have a double reward.' (Al-Bukhari).

It has been transmitted by 'Ubada, may Allah be pleased with him, that the Prophet Muhammad, may Allah bless him and grant him peace, said, 'Whoever bears witness that there is no god except Allah, alone without any partner; and that Muhammad is His slave and His Messenger; and that 'Isa is the slave of Allah and His Messenger and His Word which he bestowed on Mary and a Spirit from Him; and that the Garden is true and the Fire is true – then Allah will make him enter the Garden, however few his good actions may have been. (Al-Bukhari).

# GLOSSARY OF ARABIC TERMS

**Allah ta'Ala :** Allah the Most High, the Lord of all the worlds. Allah, the supreme and mighty Name, indicates the One, the Existent, the Creator, the Worshipped, the Lord of the Universe. Allah is the First without beginning and the Last without end and the Outwardly Manifest and the Inwardly Hidden.

**adab :** correct behaviour inward and outward, inner courtesy coming out as graciousness in right action.

**ahlu'l-dhimma :** non-Muslims living in Muslim territory and under the protection of Muslim rule by virtue of the fact that they have agreed to pay the *jizya* tax.

**ahlu'l-kitab :** the People of the Book, a term used to refer principally to the Jews and the Christians whose religions are partly based on the Books revealed to *sayyedina* Musa and *sayyedina* 'Isa, peace be on them; a term also used, by extension, to refer to any other group of people who claim to be following a Book revealed by Allah prior to the revelation of the Qur'an.

**akhira :** the next world, what is on the other side of death, the world after this world in the realm of the Unseen; it is not the life in the *barzakh*, but the life either in the *jannah* or in the *nar*.

**'alim :** a man of knowledge from amongst the Muslims who acts on what he knows.

**arwah :** the plural of *ruh*.

**ayah :** a sign, a verse of the Qur'an.

**ayat :** the plural of *ayah*.

**baraka :** a blessing, any good which is bestowed by Allah, and especially that which increases; a subtle beneficent spiritual energy which can flow through things and people or places. It is experienced in certain places more strongly than in others, and in some places and objects overpoweringly so. Its highest realm of activity is the human being. Purity permits its flow, for it is purity itself, which is Light. Density of perception blocks it. It is transformative, healing and immeasurable.

**barzakh** : an interspace between two realities which both separates and yet links them; commonly used to describe the interspace between the *dunya* and the *akhira,* which begins when death takes place, when the *ruh* leaves the body – and ends when the Last Day arrives, when the *ruh* and the body are reunited again; also used to describe the realm of the *arwah* in the Unseen, which is the abode of the *ruh* prior to its entering the unborn foetus in the womb after about sixteen weeks of pregnancy.

**dajjal** : the false Messiah whose appearance marks the imminent end of the world, the antithesis of Jesus. The science of recognising Dajjal is very intricate and carefully delineated. The manifestation will appear both as a person, and as a certain historical situation, and as a series of cosmic phenomena. Dajjal will affect the masses and cause chaos.

**deen**: the life-transaction, submission and obedience to a particular system of rules and practices, a debt of exchange between two parties, in this usage between the Creator and the created. Allah says in the Qur'an: **Surely the *deen* with Allah is Islam.** (3.19).

**dhikru'llah** : remembrance of Allah, invocation of Allah. In a general sense all *'ibada* is dhikrullah. In common usage it has come to mean invocation of Allah by repetition of His Names or particular formulae. The five pillars of Islam are its foundation. Recitation of the Qur'an is its heart, and invocation of the Single Name, Allah, is its end.

**dhimma** : obligation or contract, in particular a treaty of protection for non-Muslims living in Muslim territory.

**dinar** : a gold coin weighing approximately 4.40 gms.

**dirham** : a silver coin weighing approximately 3.08 gms.

**du'a:** making supplication to Allah, asking Allah for whatever you desire.

**dunya:** the world, not as a cosmic phenomenon but as it is experienced. It derives from a root describing those grapes which appear on the vine but which when you stretch out to pick them prove to be out of reach. Dunya takes on its actuality through attachment. When the heart is liberated, dunya disappears and *akhira*, the next invisible world – appears. Dunya is vanishing and moving away, while the next world is appearing and approaching.

**faqih** : an *'alim* with a sound knowledge of the *shari'a*, who by virtue of his knowledge is able to make a legal judgement.

**Fatiha** : the 'Opening', the opening *surah* of the Qur'an.

**fitra** : the first nature, the natural, primal condition of mankind in harmony with nature.

**fuqaha** : the plural of *faqih*.

**goy** : anyone who is not a Jew.

**goyim** : the plural of *goy*.

**ghusl** : ritual washing of the whole body with water alone in order to be pure for the prayer.

**hadith** : reported speech, particularly of, or about, the Prophet Muhammad, may Allah bless him and grant him peace.

**hadith qudsi** : those words of Allah on the tongue of His Prophet, may Allah bless him and grant him peace, which are not part of the Revelation of the Qur'an.

**hajj** : the annual pilgrimage to Makka which every Muslim who has the means should make once in a life-time; the performance of the rites of the hajj in the protected area which surrounds the Ka'ba. The hajj is one of the indispensable pillars of Islam.

**halal** : permitted by the *shari'a*.

**hanif** : naturally pure, and so only able to worship only Allah.

**haqiqa** : the truth, reality, Allah.

**haram** : forbidden by the *shari'a*; also a protected area, an inviolable place, in which certain behaviour is forbidden or necessary.

**Haramayn** : the two protected areas of *Makka* and *Madina*.

**hasan** : good.

**Hawd** : the watering-place of the Prophet Muhammad, may Allah bless him and grant him peace, whose drink will refresh those who have crossed the *Sirat* into the Garden on the Last Day.

**hijra** : emigration in the way of Allah. Islam takes its dating from the hijra of the Prophet Muhammad, may Allah bless him and grant him peace, from Makka to Madina, in 622 CE.

**'ibada** : any act of worship.

**'id** : a festival; there are two main 'Ids in the Muslim year – the 'Id al-Adha which seals the rites of the *hajj*, and the 'Id al-Fitr which marks the end of the fast of *Ramadan*.

**ihsan** : the state of being *hasan*; being absolutely sincere to Allah in oneself; it is to worship Allah as though you see Him, knowing that although you do not see Him, He sees you.

**Imam** : the one who leads the prayer, a leader who is chosen.

**iman** : acceptance, belief, trust, in Allah, a gift from Him. Iman is to believe in Allah, His angels, His revealed Books, His messengers, the Last Day, the Garden and the Fire, and that everything is by the Decree of Allah, both the good of it and the bad of it.

**Islam** : peace and submission to the will of Allah, the way of life embodied by all the Prophets, given its final form in the prophetic guidance brought by the Prophet Muhammad, may Allah bless him and grant him peace. The five pillars of Islam are the affirmation of the *shahada*, doing the *salat*, paying the *zakat*, fasting the month of *Ramadan*, and doing the *hajj* once in a life-time if you are able.

**isnad** : the record, either memorised or recorded in writing, of the names of the people who form the chain of human transmission, person to person, by means of which a *hadith* is preserved – and accordingly these people themselves. One of the sciences of the Muslims which was developed after the Prophet Muhammad's death, may Allah bless him and grant him peace, is the science of assessing the authenticity of a *hadith* by assessing the reliability of its isnad.

**'isra'** : the Night Journey of the Prophet Muhammad, may the blessings and peace of Allah be on him, from Makka to Jerusalem and then through the realms of the seven heavens beyond the limit of forms, the *sidrat al-muntaha,* to within a bow-span's length or nearer to the Presence of the Real.

**Jahannam** : one of the names of Hell.

**jahiliyyah** : the time of ignorance, before the coming of Islam.

**jannah** : the Garden, Paradise, the final destination and resting place of the *muminun* in the *akhira*.

**Jibril** : the angel Gabriel, peace be on him.

**jinn**: unseen beings created from smokeless fire who co-habit the earth together with mankind.

**jizya** : the annual tax paid by all healthy adult males of the *ahlu'l-dhimma* who are guaranteed the protection of the Muslims in return.

**Ka'ba** : the cube-shaped building at the centre of the Haram in Makka, originally built by the Prophet Ibrahim, peace be on him, and rebuilt with the help of the Prophet Muhammad, may Allah bless him and grant him peace; also known as the House of Allah. The Ka'ba is the focal point which all Muslims face when doing the *salat*. This does not mean that Allah lives inside the Ka'ba, nor does it mean that the Muslims worship the Ka'ba. It is Allah Who is worshipped and Allah is not contained or confined in any form or place or time or concept.

**kafir** : a person who commits *kufr*, an unbeliever, one who covers up the true nature of existence, the opposite of a *mumin*.

**kafirun** : the plural of *kafir*.

**Kalim** : the one to whom Allah spoke directly, meaning the Prophet Musa, peace be on him.

**Kawthar** : it is said that Kawthar is a river in the Garden, abundant blessing, intercession, and the *Hawd* of the Prophet Muhammad, may Allah bless him and grant him peace.

**khalif** : someone who stands in for someone else; in this usage, the leader of the Muslim community who stands in as the representative of Allah.

**kufr** : to cover up the truth, to reject Allah and His Messengers, may the blessings and peace of Allah be on him.

**la ilaha illa'llah** : there is no god but Allah.

**Madina** : the city, the place of the *deen*, often called Madina al-Munawarra – the illuminated, or the enlightened, city – where the revelation of the Qur'an was completed and in which the Prophet Muhammad died and is buried, may Allah bless him and grant him peace. The first Muslim community was established in Madina al-Munawarra, and Allah says in the Qur'an that this is the best community ever raised up from amongst mankind. Their hearts and intentions and actions were illuminated and enlightened and purified, may Allah be pleased with all of them, through Allah and His Messenger, and today Madina is still illuminated by the presence of the *arwah* of those of them who are buried there – especially the Messenger of Allah, may the blessings and peace of Allah be on him and them – and by the presence of those who follow in their footsteps.

**Makka** : the city in which the Ka'ba stands, and in which the Prophet Muhammad was born, may Allah bless him and grant him peace, and where the revelation of the Qur'an commenced.

**mala'ika** : the angels, who are made of light and glorify Allah unceasingly. They are neither male nor female. They do not need food or drink. They are incapable of wrong action and disobedience to Allah. They do whatever Allah commands them to do. Everyone has two recording angels with them who record their actions and none of this escapes the knowledge of Allah.

**maqam al-Ibrahim** : the station of Ibrahim, the place where the Prophet Ibrahim stood in prayer in front of the Ka'ba, peace be on him, and which marks the place of prayer following *tawaf* of the Ka'ba.

**Masjid al-Aqsa** : the 'Furthest Mosque' in Jerusalem, built in the 7th century CE, which stands where the Temple of Solomon once stood. The *qibla* of the first Muslim community in Madina was initially towards Jerusalem, until it was replaced by the *qibla* towards Makka, in 2 AH.

**Masjid Al-Haram** : the 'Protected Mosque', the name of the mosque built around the Ka'ba in the Haram at Makka.

**Masjid An-Nabiyyi** : the 'Prophet's Mosque', the name of the mosque in which is the Prophet Muhammad's tomb, may Allah bless him and grant him peace, in Madina.

**mathani** : 'often repeated', the seven mathani are usually taken to mean the seven *ayat* of Surat al-Fatiha, the opening *surah* of the Qur'an, which is repeated at least seventeen times a day by every Muslim who does the five obligatory daily prayers.

**mi'raj :** the Night Journey of the Prophet Muhammad, may the blessings and peace of Allah be on him, from Makka to Jerusalem and then through the realms of the seven heavens beyond the limit of forms, the *sidrat al-muntaha,* to within a bow-span's length or nearer to the Presence of the Real.

**Muhammad ar-Rasulu'llah :** Muhammad is the Messenger of Allah, may the blessings and peace of Allah be on him.

**muhsin:** someone who possesses the quality of *ihsan,* who remembers Allah constantly.

**mumin:** a believer, someone who possesses the quality of *iman,* who trusts in Allah and accepts His Messenger, may Allah bless him and grant him peace, and for whom the *akhira* is more real than the *dunya.* The mumin longs for the Garden so much, that this world seems like the Fire by comparison.

**muminun :** the plural of *mumin.*

**munafiq :** a hypocrite; the hypocrites amongst the Muslims outwardly profess Islam on the tongue, but inwardly reject Allah and His Messenger, may Allah bless him and grant him peace, siding with the *kafirun* against the Muslims. The deepest part of the Fire is reserved for the *munafiqun.*

**munafiqun:** the plural of *munafiq.*

**mushrik :** one who commits *shirk.*

**mushrikin :** the plural of *mushrik.*

**Muslim:** whoever follows the way of Islam, doing what is obligatory, avoiding what is forbidden, keeping within the limits prescribed by Allah, following the *sunnah* of the Prophet Muhammad, may Allah bless him and grant him peace, in what he or she is able. A Muslim is, by definition, one who is safe and sound, at peace in this world and promised the Garden in the next world.

**nabi** : a Prophet, a rightly-guided man sent by Allah to guide others how to live and how to only worship Allah.

**nafila** : a voluntary act of *'ibada* .

**nar** : the Fire of Jahannam, Hell, the final destination and place of torment of the *kafirun* and the *munafiqun* in the *akhira*.

**nifaq** : hypocrisy.

**qadar** : the decree of Allah, which determines every sub-atomic particle in existence, and accordingly whatever appears to be in existence. One of Allah's Names is 'al-Qadir' – 'the Powerful, the One Who does what He wants, the One Who has Power over everything'. The Prophet Muhammad, may Allah bless him and grant him peace, said, 'Everything is by decree.' (*Al-Muwatta'* of *Imam* Malik: 46.1.5).

**qibla** : the direction faced in prayer, which, for the Muslims, is towards the Ka'ba in Makka. Everyone has a direction in life, but only the Muslims have this *qibla*.

**qintar** : a relatively large measure of weight, about 45 kgs.

**Qur'an** : the 'Recitation', the last Revelation from Allah to mankind and the *jinn* before the end of the world, revealed to the Prophet Muhammad, may Allah bless him and grant him peace, through the angel Jibril, over a period of twenty-three years, the first thirteen of which were spent in Makka and the last ten of which were spent in Madina. The Qur'an amends, encompasses, expands, surpasses and abrogates all the earlier revelations revealed to the earlier Messengers, peace be on all of them. The Qur'an is the greatest miracle given to the Prophet Muhammad by Allah, for he was illiterate and could neither read nor write. The Qur'an is the uncreated word of Allah. The Qur'an still exists today exactly as it was originally revealed, without any alteration or change or addition or deletion. Whoever recites the Qur'an with courtesy and sincerity receives knowledge and wisdom, for it is the well of wisdom in this age.

**rak'a :** a unit of the prayer, a complete series of standing, bowing, prostrations and sittings.

**rak'at :** the plural of *rak'a*.

**Ramadan :** the month of fasting, the ninth month in the Muslim lunar calendar, during which all adult Muslims who are in good health fast from the first light of dawn until sunset each day. The Qur'an was first revealed in the month of Ramadan. The fast of Ramadan is one of the indispensable pillars of Islam.

**rasul :** a Messenger, often a *nabi* who was given a revealed Book by Allah.

**ruh :** the spirit which gives life, formed from pure light; also the angel Jibril.

**sahih :** healthy and sound with no defects; often used to describe a fully authenticated *hadith*. Two of the most reliable collections of *hadith*, those of Al-Bukhari and Muslim, are both called 'the Sahih'.

**sajda :** the act of making prostration, particularly in the prayer (*salat* – see below).

**Salaf :** the 'early years', a term used generally to describe the early generations of the Muslims, particularly the *sahaba*, the companions of the Messenger of Allah, may the blessings and peace of Allah be on him and them.

**salat :** the prayer, particularly the five daily obligatory ritual prayers of the Muslims which consist of fixed numbers of *rak'at* in worship to Allah. Salat is one of the indispensable pillars of Islam.

**sawm :** fasting, particularly the fast of Ramadan, from food and drink – and making love if you are married – during daylight, from the first light of dawn until sunset.

**sayyedina :** 'our master', a term of respect.

**shahada** : to witness, to bear witness that: There is no god but Allah and that Muhammad is the Messenger of Allah, may Allah bless him and grant him peace. The shahada is the gateway to Islam in this world and the gateway to the Garden in the next world. It is easy to say, but to act on it is a vast undertaking which has far-reaching consequences, both in inward awareness and in outward action, both in this world and in the next world. Continual affirmation of the shahada is one of the indispensable pillars of Islam.

**shari'a** : a road, the legal and social modality of a people based on the revelation of their Prophet. The last shari'a in history is that of Islam. It abrogates all previous shari'as. It is, being the last, therefore the easiest to follow, for it is applicable to the whole human race wherever they are.

**shaykh** : an old man – an *'alim* who has knowledge of Allah and His Messenger, may Allah bless him and grant him peace, and His *deen* – the one who guides you from knowledge of your self to knowledge of your Lord.

**shaytan** : a devil, particularly Iblis (Satan), an evil *jinn* who prompts mankind and the *jinn* to rebel against Allah. Shaytan is part of the creation of Allah, and we seek refuge in Allah from the evil that He has created.

**shayatin** : the plural of *shaytan.*

**shirk** : the unforgivable wrong action of worshipping something or someone other than Allah or associating something or someone as a partner with Him; the opposite of *Tawhid* which is affirmation of Divine Unity. Shirk is idol-worship, which is attributing form to Allah by attempting to confine Him within an object, a concept, a ritual or a myth – whereas Allah is not like anything and has no form. He cannot be conceived of or perceived.

**sidrat al-muntaha**: 'the lote-tree of the furthest limit', the place where form ends.

**Sirat** : the narrow bridge which must be crossed on the Last Day in order to enter the Garden.

**Sirat al-Mustaqim** : the Straight Path, of Islam, which leads through this world to the Garden in the next world.

**sunnah**: a form, the customary practice of a person or group of people. It has come to refer almost exclusively to the practice of the Messenger of Allah, Muhammad, may Allah bless him and grant him peace, but also comprises the customs of the first generation of Muslims in Madina, who acted in accordance with what they had learned from him and who transmitted what they had learned to the next generation. The sunnah is a complete behavioural science that has been systematically kept outside the learning framework of this society, but which nevertheless has been preserved by those to whom it has been transmitted and who continue to embody it as their way of life. The Messenger of Allah, may Allah bless him and grant him peace, said: "I have left two matters with you. As long as you hold to them, you will not go the wrong way. They are the Book of Allah and the Sunnah of His Prophet." (*Al-Muwatta'* of *Imam* Malik: 46.1.3).

**surah** : a form, a chapter of the Qur'an, composed of *ayat* linked by thematic content.

**tafsir** : commentary on the Qur'an.

**taqwa** : being careful, knowing your place in the cosmos. Its proof is the experience of awe of Allah, which inspires a person to be on guard against wrong action and eager for actions which are pleasing to Him.

**tawaf** : circling the Ka'ba; tawaf is done in sets of seven circuits followed by two *rak'at* of prayer, preferably at the *maqam al-Ibrahim.*

**tawba** : returning to correct action after error, turning away from wrong action to Allah and asking His Forgiveness, turning to face the Real whereas before one turned one's back. Your turning to Him is in reality His turning to you.

**Tawhid** : the Divine Unity, Unity in its most profound sense. Allah is One in His Essence and His Attributes and His Acts. The whole of the creation and what it contains is one unified event which in itself has no lasting reality. Allah is the Real: **Surely we come from Allah and surely to Him we return.** (Qur'an: 2.156).

**'ulama'** : the plural of *'alim.*

**Ummah** : a nation, the body of Muslims as one distinct community.

**'umrah** : the lesser pilgrimage to the Ka'ba in Makka and the performance of its rites in the protected area which surrounds the Ka'ba. You can go on 'umrah at any time of the year.

**wahi** : revelation; the inspiration placed in the hearts and the minds of the Prophets, may the blessings and peace of Allah be on all of them, by Allah ta'Ala.

**wudu** : ritual washing of the hands, mouth, nostrils, face, forearms, head, ears and feet with water alone so as to be pure for the prayer. It is necessary to be in *ghusl* for wudu to be effective.

**Yawm al-Qiyama** : the Day of Standing, the Last Day, when everyone who has ever lived will be given life again, their actions and intentions in this world weighed in the balance, and their final abode determined; also known as 'Yawm al-Ba'ath' – the Day of Rising, 'Yawm al-Hashr' – the Day of Gathering, 'Yawm al-Qiyama' – the Day of Standing, 'Yawm al-Mizan' – the Day of the Balance, 'Yawm al-Hisab' – the Day of Reckoning, 'Yawm ad-Deen' – the Day of the Life-Transaction, and 'Yawm al-Akhira' – the Day of the Next World. The Last Day will be followed by life in the Garden or the Fire, for ever.

**zakat** : the wealth tax obligatory on Muslims each year, usually payable in the form of one fortieth of surplus wealth which is more than a certain fixed minimum amount, which is called the *nisab.* Zakat is payable on accumulated wealth, especially gold and silver, merchandise, certain crops, certain livestock, and on subterranean and mineral wealth. As soon as zakat is collected it is redistributed to those in need, as defined in the Qur'an and the *hadith*. Zakat is one of the indispensable pillars of Islam.

**zakat al-fitr** : a small obligatory head-tax imposed on every responsible Muslim who has the means for himself and his dependants. It is paid once yearly near the end of Ramadan just before the *'Id al-Fitr*.

**Zamzam** : the well in the Haram of Makka which has the best water in the world!